The War Outside Ireland

The War Outside Ireland

a novel by
Michael Joyce

TINKERS DAM PRESS
Jackson, Michigan • Pago Pago

TINKERS DAM PRESS
1703 East Michigan Avenue
Jackson, Michigan 49202

Library of Congress Cataloging in Publication Data
Joyce, Michael, 1945-
 The war outside Ireland.
 I. Title
PS3560.0885W3   813'.54   82-80497
                              AACR2

Printed in the United States of America

2 3 4 5 6 7 8 9

For my families

In his case, though, it was part of a family pattern.
Over the years, his family had turned ironical and
lost its gift for action. It was an honorable and
violent family, but gradually the violence had been
deflected and turned inward.

Walker Percy, *The Last Gentleman*

Be secret and exult,
Because of all things known
That is most difficult.

William Butler Yeats, "To A Friend
Whose Work Has Come To Nothing"

The War Outside Ireland

A History of the Doyles in North America
With an account of their migrations

geography
and primitive peoples

The war was there before us, waiting like a once inhabited island, a clear and distant kingdom wanting to be discovered again. We landed roughly at its outskirts and walked only a little inland, but while we were there we accounted ourselves well, I think. Or at least as well as any Irish could, considering our disinclination toward struggles.

For we fought at disadvantage. The enemy hardly showed itself and so we holed up and quarreled among us in the great tradition of our race. The first shot, as it were, was my brother Jimmy's. Like so many Limmerick Rapparees, Dublin Volunteers, and Derry Provos before him, he barricaded himself for a last stand, winning what he could before he retreated.

The last shot belonged to my father. It was a hurried, tragic, and well-meaning blast fired as he escaped his also traditional bonds. He too won what he could.

And then we set sail again. Meanwhile the war continues,

inside and out, with and without us, as it always has. It is, as I say, a crystal kingdom, a floating isle, a happy space.

But you really do have to know so much before you can truly begin to understand.

Where my family now lives, the Indians lived. Seneca Indians of the Iroquois nation, they filled a spiral village of muddy streets, longhouses brimming with dogs and smoky women in stained cotton, some toothless, smoking pipes. Their children lived in the mud ruts, wily and swift as rats, playing dice and sticking birds with pointed sticks. Shrieking, silent, or singing, they avoided the missionary church, drifted in the lazy hours of thick August afternoons to the trading post, the store, where the men could be found.

Mostly the men drank whiskey but not in the way we've invented the myth. No, drinking slowly, like the Indians I remember from my own youth, distant Mohawks, steel-working men, silent drinkers like the Irish also are. My father drinks that way now that his brother is dead. Now that he drinks only when the pain exceeds patience. Now that there is no one to talk to.

The only outward reminders of the Indian presence are the name of the road that intersects ours—Indian Church—and the small park where we played baseball and hunted black walnuts over the graves of long-dead Iroquois. When I think of it now, the hill we sledded on, making lean-to's in its valley in warmer months, must have been the northern limit of the village, the last slope before the flatland to the Buffalo River. I have a dim memory of roasting potatoes over the coals of a fire we made in that valley. "Mickys," they were, charred things, salted heavily, sweet where they were undercooked. We were grubby Irish children and as loud as Indians.

My father once showed me the abstract of title for our house. The Indian spirals had been platted over by later Indians and deeded to an Iroquois fraternal society with an unmemorable name, something too much like the names of service organizations that beef up business men's obituaries. There was some connection with the past in that photocopied document but my sister Deidre's news about our village supplied much more.

We lived on land designated by the Iroquois nation for outcasts, criminals, and mad warriors—the poor and anti-social. Deidre, who has studied Amerindians at Harvard, found this. The story goes something like this.

The men at the store squatted or crouched on a long porch, hooded from the sun but outside still—the kind of wide and long porch the neighborhood still has, and our house had until the concrete slab and aluminum replaced it. The whiskey was in bottles dark as the skin on the hands that passed it. Inside the store an Indian agent of a protestant commerce stewarded a complicated economy: barrels of beans and flour and gunpowder, rancid butter packed under ice and hay, bolts of gaudy cotton hung on wires from the ceiling. Knives filled glass cases like iron fish, and leather hung to tan in an outer storeroom. The dogs waited by this door to catch and chew the few rats that dared the light. Most of the village business was accomplished on this porch, the tribal longhouse having long become just ceremonial.

Among these men there were certainly still those who remembered the wars. Men without an eye or ear, flesh scarred in white rills from knives or bullets, sullenly angry with change. Bad men and good men, they spat gobs of brown through brown teeth. There are still such men in this part of South Buffalo; they remember wars and drink whiskey, they spit and grow fat or lean. None stay the same.

Among the Seneca men on a given day there might have been the brother-in-law of Mary Jemison, he, a common criminal and a specific murderer. Mary Jemison was a legend, a kind of saint. A white woman taken in by these wonderfully fierce people but staying calm with it, like one of those children suckled by wolves. She became a woman of influence, a mediatrix and landholder, her land eventually given over to a state park, her mediating role lost to legend. There is a museum to her memory in the park now. There, her implements and most common possessions are kept behind dusty velvet ropes in a sham longhouse. The gaps between the logs have been stuffed with mortar and the windows covered with iron screening to keep out vandals.

What Deidre discovered was that Mary Jemison's brother-in-law lived in our section of the village, the outskirts, banished there because he could not forget brutal ways. Since the Seneca were especially brutal, it would have left him with a long memory. I remember Jesuits in my Jesuit high school telling how the Iroquois gnawed Isaac Jogues' fingers and quartered him alive. The Indians learned this, of course, to suit the British, perhaps the most brutal race to ever populate the earth. It was the British who established the custom of accounting death by means of scalps, paying bounty on human heads as they did on beaver pelt. Their civility is and was brutal.

I think that the criminality of the land, its outskirt's history, may explain why the original deed to our property was so corporate. The fraternal society must have developed bad land for investment when no one else would own its history. I think now of Mary Jemison's brother-in-law as I sit in the night next to my mute father on the slab porch, watching his cigarette arc into the darkness as it leaves his hand, thinking I must learn to talk to him before he dies, thinking if I had known the history of the land we sit upon, I would have taken him more seriously a year ago. I sat then in the same place, thinking then too that I must learn to talk to him, and heard him explain calmly how he could murder the nineteen year old girl who is my youngest brother Jimmy's friend and lover.

Now my father too is an outcast, not only from his family but also from the neighbors whom I hear laughing from their porches in the summer night—perhaps laughing at him, at us—and from all the citizens of the City of Buffalo, County of Erie, State of New York, who are protected from his proximate presence by the terms of his probationary sentence. Jailed on his own porch.

Even now, as my father sips his whiskey and lights another menthol cigarette, we can hear her laughing, can hear the both of them. He said a year ago he could kill the girl because she was killing my mother with the way she clung to Jimmy. Now they sit together in the kitchen, brought closer by the tragedy which I cannot help but think my own silence made me an accomplice to.

I think I'll begin by asking him about the whiskey, asking if he's in pain. But then he goes in, as I knew he would, driven away not so much by their laughing, nor by my silence, as by his residual sense of place, and the way he enforces his own sentence. And also by his project; he's spending this year in exile working in earnest on the family genealogy that he's been researching for years, working now on the Irish documents, lately arrived.

Doyles have always lived in outskirts. The main branch of the family is from the Connaught, the rocky northwest edge of Ireland, including Galway, Mayo, and Sligo. A country of poets and the slightly mad. I stopped there on my honeymoon. A sign advertised a bed-and-breakfast run by Dennis Doyle, himself a sinewy old man, the body elastic as my father's was until he had to retire and grew his pot belly.

The country was yawning grey rock, rock fields bordered by stone fences, purple heather growing in awesome meadows of contoured rock, and razor cliffs stubbled with boulders and overlooking a stone-blue sea. Badlands, but beautiful as agates, silent and hazily surreal. We were only stopping for coffee, but Dennis Doyle was out of the same and boiled up water for bovril. Then he made my new wife sit with his old wife while he walked me about the property, crossing over three fields of dust and yellow grass where the sheep chewed down to the sea coast. He discovered that I was living in New York City and asked if I might know his son, a cop in Brooklyn, then came to the point and offered to sell me one hundred acres, including the cliff we stood upon, for a hundred dollars an acre. I think now it was a good deal, as good a price as anyone will ever be offered for a section of the moon.

When we came back to the cottage, Dennis tried to convince us to stay the night, but we were bound for Sligo, to visit the grave of orange Yeats among its Celtic crosses. When he saw this huckstering wouldn't succeed, he took another tack and brought out the missus' scarves, each hand-loomed of untreated wool, draping them around my wife's neck until I bought one to save her from suffocation.

As we left, he wished us, "Good health and children," only that. But then just before we drove off, he ran out into the yard to wave us down, handing me three shillings through the window, "Because the woman says I overcharged ye." I've told my father about this Doyle but I cannot remember what town we were near and so the information didn't help him. My mother says he sounded like our Doyles.

But ours are from Drumcondra, a neat suburb of Dublin. That much my father knows for certain. I remember Drumcondra also, another bed-and-breakfast there, convenient by bus or long walk to Dublin.

Dublin fades into Drumcondra. North of the North Circular Road there's a rise and then open spaces of colleges, convents, orphanages and an asylum. Where we stayed neat houses fronted Drumcondra Road, a generally treeless path like the avenues of Buffalo are now that the elms are dead and gone. The room we shared smelled of grease from a nearby fish and chips, and there was a particularly gory Jesus of the Sacred Heart that my wife turned to the wall but could not avoid dreaming about.

The Doyles, my grandfather's grandfather, lived closer still to the center city, on St. Joseph's Road between two tram tracks and near the prison. My father says their house was a rebel post in the Easter Rebellion, but he has no way of knowing. We had none of this information when I was there so I can't say I saw St. Joseph's Road, although for convenience of memory I recall a street we came upon, wandering on our way into Dublin. There my wife was terribly frightened.

6

It was a tight little cul-de-sac of brick councilhouses, a box canyon of Irish urban renewal teeming with children: their poor polished apple faces like the MacIntoshes my mother always bought, dull red and yellow. All of them wore square brown shoes of scuffed leather, even the dingy skirted girls with hanging lace slips who called jumprope. We wandered in like deer into a shopping mall, awkward and loosely frightened. The boys, murderous innocent Dublin urchins with rough corduroy trousers, were playing a variety of dodge-ball against an inner corner. A few smaller boys danced as the ball hurtled past them or crippled them, the older boys playing the vectors of the corner with a practiced shooting gallery calm.

I know all those children shouted, and may even have sung, but I remember it in exceeding stillness. I think the girls noticed us first, the jumprope falling slack, a smaller girl hiding behind her older sister, the older sister's face pasty white with the dark wide eyes that you still see in war photos from Belfast. The boys too then stopped playing. They moved in on us like a slow, stagnant tide, circling warily. A dusty dog appeared from nowhere, its hind flanks spotted with mange. Mary's hand squeezed mine tightly, but we kept walking. I recall the dusty, dry feel in my throat as I mouthed a pleasant, "Hello!" The dog, which had been silent until then, growled in a frightened way, then tucked tail and went off. A boy touched my wife's arm, then pulled his hand away quickly.

"Is sad ilk?" he asked, his voice cherubic, but sly.

I, of course, did not understand him. In fact, I thought he was speaking Gaelic. I went through Ireland listening for Gaelic and never heard it til Connaught.

"She doesn't understand you," I answered. "We neither of us do."

Mary squeezed my hand once more, this time roughly. She was shutting me up, her voice had a sharpness to make that clear. Her fear had left her.

"Of course I understand him!" she said. She let go of me and squatted down next to the boy. There was a bruise like dried jam on his forehead above one eye. She was very near to his face, and the other children crowded even closer.

"No, it's not silk at all," she said gently, almost whispering. "It's rayon or something like that. Why? Do you like it?"

You could see the boy's eyes melt, going watery like a fish's in a bin of ice. She was seducing the little mug, his scalp turned fiery red.

Suddenly, a younger, bold-faced boy shouted from the mob behind the first boy. He sang out at the top of his lungs, his voice giddy with his own hilarious notion, a tough and joyful castrati voice.

"Naw, he t'aught it was a bloody sow's arse!"

One or two of the smaller boys laughed along with him, and he had begun to dance a step or two with the glee of his witty rejoinder when a girl shut them all up, whapping the squealer on the side of his head. His ear turned red as flannel and he seized it with a howl, weeping in the same high voice. He ran off like the dog had, sounding like a retreating ambulance.

"He's the sow of the lot," the girl said to Mary. Then she curtsied to her—actually curtsied—and begged forgiveness.

"Begging yer pardon Madam," she said, "he thought you was a social worker . . ."

"Yeah, or a prottie," a smaller boy piped in.

"But yer only American," the girl said quietly. "Aren't you?"

Mary nodded.

"Well, himself is only a dirty Doyle," the girl said, "and there's the real sow's arse, beggin yer pardon."

With that the boys snorted and broke away, running back to their game, while a few of the older girls stood their ground, laughing and saying, "Hear." Mary talked with them awhile, but I watched the boys. I was hoping that young Doyle would reappear, and once even thought I spotted him, looking down on us from a window of one of the antiseptic brick houses, his eyes still red with ignominy. Even now I wish there had been some way to tell him that, if his scorn was for what the girl said it was for, we forgive him entirely.

For it is all a sow's arse sometimes. And it's a wise boy who can tell silk from corporate piggy rot.

Doyle never reappeared. The girls asked Mary to skip rope

with them, but she declined, saying I was in a hurry to be off to Dublin. She was right about me, though I've felt since that it was wrong to rush her off when she didn't want to.

We spent that afternoon studying the two open volumes of the Book Of Kells on display under glass at Trinity. Or rather say that I did, for Mary tired quickly and went out to sit in the quadrangle, returning to gather me up when they were closing the library. A student, she said, had come and flirted with her for an hour, asking first to paint her portrait and finally to take her out for a pint of stout. I had identified a series of identical faces in the periphery of the large illuminated letter on display, the faces looking like young Doyle. We each counted the afternoon a success.

Years later, two months to the day after our son was born, I had a dream of Dublin, quite clear and exact. Those same street kids and our Thomas a toddler. They taught him to dance, and then Mary and I danced with him. It was a lovely dream, the light like honey and the children were clean as sparrows. Thomas laughed and laughed.

I walked in and out of the streets of this Indian village, this Drumcondra, at dusk, starting off on Indian Church and winding in and back among the side streets, Hillside and Oshawa. And here, too, it seemed exceedingly still, although I am sure—Mary always talks of it—it is noisy to excess. How to describe this neighborhood? There is a momentary question in my mind whether the neighborhood seems Irish because we Irish lived here, or whether we Irish lived here because it seemed so; but that does not seem to matter.

The stillness comes from the trees, which, despite what I've said about the elms, remain. Mostly now they are maples, dropping whirleybirds into the buttery light. However a few obnoxious cottonwoods—the cost of living near a creek, I tell my mother—send off their seed stuff like alien intelligences. It settles like dry snow, which the urchins here light along the gutters, watching it burn.

9

There are still elms, though not in the thickness I grew in, when we seemed to play in dark tunnels when we ran through the streets. And chestnut trees, two I remember especially; we gathered and waxed the nuts, threaded shoe strings through them to play a game called kingers, banging them against each other until one broke. A fool might say that we grew in a similar way, banged against each other until breaking. I think perhaps my father would understand that, if I could talk to him.

The second cause of the silence is closeness. The lots are small and the houses are large, all of them on our block rising up three full stories and then another attic story to a peak like an inverted ship's prow. When my brother-in-law painted ours (the first time in the twenty years we've lived here), he hung from a bosun's chair with the other end of the rope run straight over the house and tied to the neighbor's car in their driveway. My brother-in-law is a stocky, fat man, with a kind face and a kind self, a face like an owl's; he hung there like an ox in a parachute, the brush flapping white paint against the peak.

Blocks of these high pointed houses run into each other like hotel hallways, the houses grey or brown mostly and often sided in the tar paper that is meant to look like brick but never does. They are so close together that once in my teens when I decided that my chevrolet could make it to the backyard despite all warning, I shredded the skin off my knuckles where they gripped the lip of the roof outside the driver's side window.

At least half the houses (nearly all on Indian Church, where they are double-wide) are split into flats, each flat five or six rooms and a kitchen. Always there are porches, top and bottom, like bunkbeds. These flats are filled with the families of the working class unbeknownst to themselves: Champion, Barbaritz, Doyle, Reich, Bascal, Kelly, and Mahony—which is as far as I can remember on our side only, and that list is only a third of the families on our side of the street. Boys play dodge-ball like Dublin kids (turning on, and disposing with, the girls where they chance to play); cars choke and jolt, cough blue, growl down the block; a beefy girl pushes herself on a skateboard, then later (what she will grow into), a short, beefy, sensual woman and her cluster of children come down with a shopping cart. I can see imprinted on her face the hungry, workmanlike, brief, intense, sexuality of her life; five kids around her and another in the belly. This street has always flowed with kids, bubbling up like a spring from mud. Our family too, the four and four, boys and girls, men and women.

The whole neighborhood is a wash of anarchy and dark places: sputtering mowers on blanket-sized lawns, grasses elsewhere grown through and over the concrete; those same narrow driveways where dusk comes by mid-afternoon, the garages behind them ripe for sexual play, gangs of boys breathing like horses. A deeply, darkly, Catholic sexual place; so madly loud that the first time we brought our baby here, visiting from Japan, he squealed in delight at the excess of it, laughing on the porch like the whole thing was a show for him, while before me on a small table my coffee sat next to an open can of motorcycle oil which nobody there claimed to own.

What I am saying is that it is exactly because it is so loud, so alive, so dark, so leafy, so buzzingly, watery excessive there, that the silence at certain times—morning or dusk, the traditional eating times—is like a girl in a garage taking her clothes off. Or—since that is hopelessly out of date, with even the lower classes liberated—like some lost sense of furtive flesh, girls in the park, or bedrooms with no one home, or motels, or wherever they take them, Jimmy could tell me.

In the noise of this place, the silence is made flesh and dwells momentarily among us. That sexual silence is what I love here; is why (the people aside, say if they didn't live here) I do come back from the serenity and motorized madness of the orient where I live now.

But it is also why I have come to hate them: English, protties, social workers, steel plant, the whole sow's arse of them, whoever and everybody it was who brought quiet, which is something unlike silence, something ordered and juiceless. They brought my father to hate it all, to think it was taking his wife from him, to turn on a mad black-Irish girl whose only sin was being close enough to blame, closer than the downtown lawyers and bankers with their hormonal pills and scented soap, their legal, civil church and their exile of probationary quiet. Her only sin was being her wild-eyed, Crazy Jane poet self, all noise and silence come out from the garages, out from under the bridges in the park, out from the Siren shore, to take poor Jimmy. Who wanted it that way. We Doyle men liking in our own way to be wooed instead of wooing, as did the Iroquois before us here.

Here in Japan I live in a dry well, a stone cylinder, which is cool, mossy, and thick as death or sleep. It is really not a well, of course, but a stone house, covered with a stucco paste of stone; but when I return here, as after each of the times—both these summers—when I went to Buffalo, once for Jimmy's first crisis, again for my father's trial, the house even smells like wells do, of stale water and green plants. Lovely.

I am a late sleeper, an endless sleeper sometimes, yet here alone, here in Japan, I rise early, awakened by the smell of ice at sunrise. I breakfast on seaweed and grain noodles, but I do not enjoy tea, not being pure enough to ingest it. But my wife and the baby thrive on it.

We live in the country here, although the country, like everything, grows smaller. All here is motorized, mechanized, growing in on itself like the box canyon of the councilhouses in Drumcondra. Even the meadow which sits next to our house has the sense of something electronic, programmed to this peacefulness. For the Japanese have an oddly distracted sense about the green of open space, whether formal city gardens or the meadow next to us with its odd and gigantic horses. The Japanese do not seem to notice the space any-more; or perhaps it is only one of the many secrets they keep.

More likely, they are too busy motorizing things. Even now, ground squirrels cross the road endlessly when we drive out here from the city, and they seem electrical, small transistors. I've never struck one so I do not know what fills them, but a week ago I could not avoid driving over a rabbit, the only one I've ever seen here. Its bloody fur still remains on the undercarriage of my station wagon. A small clot of red stains the enamel like a miniature landscape. I prayed for the rabbit's soul and made an offering of rice. In the white offering bowl, a forest of blue-green mold has grown from the darkened grains. It too is a landscape, a morning vision, pointillist pines.

It is ironically easier to remember here the peacefulness of walking through my neighborhood in Buffalo. And to help when I cannot remember, I have an instamatic photograph, itself a memory. The photo shows my father and me on the porch, the row of houses down the block disappearing into perspective and the edge of the frame. The picture captures not the image but the cone of space from its foreground to the apex of the camera. Thus the action of viewing it becomes a plastic art, the imagination of space.

The Japanese have designed into this camera centuries of wisdom. It captures what is there but is not there. For there is an economy of array, of what is eternally and simply there, despite our presences. This, too, the Japanese have used to success. It is their aesthetic: three pines stand behind my house, each different, each suiting the others. They also slice the wind in winter.

The photograph was taken in the rain; the house and its neighbors are misty gentle, secure in their time. I almost want to hold the photo to my ear, to listen to the long, indelicate rhythm of it, its pattern woven as surely as sound, the crinoline softness of a single word rustling under it all. Home.

I choose to think of it at dusk, without rain, a summer night. The cottonwood are there again, drifting, drifting, so many of the wispy seeds that I think this species must have the lowest of fertility indices. Seed after seed after seed drifts, and still there are only the three old trees. How completely unlike this neighborhood, the people of home, who are nothing if they are not fecund.

Even in the after dinner silence, there are people whose eyes chart my every step. Only one child is out, a boy making his way warily along the cracked sidewalk where the maple roots have heaved the concrete blocks up against each other like shelves of ice. He watches me carefully, not at all friendly. It is unusual here to walk on any street but one's own, unusual to walk at all unless you are old, infirm, or a regular drunk. Or a child, of course.

Looking up from his face, I see someone else watching me from an upper porch, a man with yellow skin, his round and bony shoulders jutting from his strap-undershirt. He drinks from a can of beer, but his eyes watch me until I pass into someone else's eyes. He could be my father; my father would come home from the plant and sit on the porch in his undershirt, drinking beers, trying to forget the furnaces. There is no question of talking to this man, even though our eyes have met directly. He also is trying to forget, perhaps forget that I am there. I try to walk very carefully along the cracked and heaved squares of his sidewalk, being mindful not to step into the rag grass at his edges, onto his lawn. The walking becomes a dance, an attempt at balance, and I imagine I can hear the man suck disgusted at his can of beer, smirking at my effeteness. I however know that, in walking at least, I am an artist, and I accept that. It gives currency to my smallness, to the intricacy of my emotions, especially my grief. People comment on how I walk.

But then I am free of the man with the yellow skin and eyes, walking freely, artistically, along the shady silence of the street. It is a child's dream, walking along the concrete among these grey houses and eyes, a dream of walking off into the perspective of a drawing, to the place where the two lines narrow and then meet like in the instamatic photograph of my father and myself. I think I could dissolve gently into a point, and then remember (shocked!) this was what Jimmy feared in his first crisis. Dissolving, becoming a mere jot.

14

There are always the eyes to retrieve you, I should have told him that. Back there in the silence, in the darkness, ours is a neighborhood of eyes. It is this way even at night, at all hours of the day. There is always someone awake in our neighbor-hood, always someone watching. You can be walking down a street at night, right into the center of the dark valley between the street lights, and find yourself staring into the thickness of a porch, a black oblong of shapeless space. Suddenly, in the center of the darkness, there is a pulse of orange light (or two: like the eyes of a fox), as someone sucks a cigarette in. Watching.

We are like owls here, like Iroquois, my family especially. Grogginess is a family rhythm. All our days, especially now when I visit and turn my habits upside down, are spent groggy and abstract. The whole family wakes at noon and waits until dinner. It was always so. Going to school we went in a grog; my mother woke only long enough to get us off, then went back to sleep. In afternoons, we would eat. It was more so to while away the time until dinner than to satisfy hunger, although someone could say that for us the passing of time was a hunger. After dinner the long talking of the table would continue, extending into night, the cool dark house, the huge dark porch.

The talk itself was common, mindless or of one undiffer-entiated mind, an endless murmur and babble, rising and falling like a sea. It was another set of eyes in that we were inside it and everything else was outside. I was always either looking out or going out the door as a kid, I do so even now when we return. For the door is the territory of a map; what's there, what isn't. Another outskirts.

The way we talked and watched all night it would seem that our family had tropic roots, coastal Sardinian or Greek, rather than the cold Irish sea rocks, or the German northness of my mother's side.

You'd think we would have seen it coming, you'd think the whole village of us would have seen it, whatever it was, the decline of the west or the way they used us up, the protties and the English. But then you'd have thought the Iroquois would have seen it, although some say maybe they did.

Sometimes things get so crowded, so busy, that you can't see anything; or you see everything and there's nothing to do about what is coming. I was thinking of this the other night when I drove out to the supermarket. The parking lot was empty, or nearly so; all-night stores seem something the Japanese have adopted for prestige more than convenience. They like to have Western ways. For the first time I noticed that the supermarket was bounded by a field, an open space, seeming vastly more open without the thousands of Datsuns, Toyotas, and Hondas. I saw also that except for the ideogram characters of the banners pasted on the windows, I could have been anywhere in America. I wasn't surprised to think this, but I was surprised that it was true. What I think so infrequently is.

I was still thinking as I stood in the surprisingly long line for check-out, holding two packs of ramen noodles in my hand. There was a young woman behind me, wearing cheap plastic sandals and California-style powder-blue slacks. She was obviously from out of our district, you could tell it in her accent as she chatted with and complained to the old man in line behind her.

"They have stores like this where I come from," she was saying. "But in Detroit, they have enough help on duty to avoid these long lines. In Detroit, people shop at night. There are always cars in the lots, and help in the stores."

She was from Tokyo; Tokyo people have a sense of humor, they call their city Detroit. She was talking to me now.

"You like those things?" she asked, her bird-thin finger touching the cellophane of my noodles. "You like them better than Campbells? They have Campbells here you know."

I answered her politely. Here, one always speaks politely to women, especially at night. I said I did like them.

"Takes too much time," she said. "That's what's best about American food, how quick it is."

"There's more time here in Japan," I said.

16

"I guess there is," she said. "Looking at this line, it seems like there is." She laughed. "Japan's as good a name as any for it. You wait and wait forever here, waiting for nothing. In Detroit it's different."

She had become mysteriously angry as she spoke, nearly spitting out the last words. It was very unladylike the way she talked, her voice crass and loud like all big-city women. Yet everyone in the line remained remote, no one took notice of her, everyone stayed polite and quiet. Even as she dropped the six-pack of beer she had been carrying and pushed her way through the line and out the door, no one said a word.

You could see the headlights as she drove toward the store on her way out of the nearly deserted lot. For a moment I thought she was going to drive straight through the large window; the lights speared toward us, growing painfully bright. But then she turned, the little red eyes of the Datsun disappearing, and only the previously invisible empty field was left there beyond the window.

I wanted to say something to the cashier about the woman, wanted really I think to apologize for her. Instead I nodded to him in silence, handing him the six-pack from the floor as if it were a lost purse that I had found.

That night, as I went to sleep, it was maddening to think of the horses asleep in the darkness next to our house. Invisible horses, their bellies full of grass, the stale water in their trough augmented by the day's rain, I heard them whinny in their curious Japanese way. They sounded frightened. Perhaps they had seen the spirit of the dead rabbit; perhaps the witch spirit from Detroit had followed me home. Perhaps they saw that something was coming to fill all the empty spaces, black parachutes falling through black sky, filling their meadow as certainly as the field next to the all-night supermarket. Or perhaps they merely wanted to talk.

early history

I think my brothers think we've always lived there, in the Iroquois village. The missing spokes from the bannister on the upstairs landing must seem to them the expression of a toothless friendly relation—an uncle or someone—the benevolent guardian deity of the house. A frightening, clownish face, like one of those Shinto spirits with white face and mop-rope hair, meant to keep away bad luck.

Bad luck had struck that first summer. Seventeen year old Jimmy, the youngest of us four brothers, went into some sort of swoon in the bathroom and he wouldn't come out or speak. At least he wouldn't speak sense.

I think I remember when the bannister was whole, just after we came to Drumcondra, the oak spindles with their multiple feminine turnings, the caresses of the lathe, intact. The wood had a fatty burnish before it was covered over with each of the three repaintings. Sandlewood, cream, and celery. I think I may have dislodged the first of the two spindles myself, perhaps to use for a streetball bat.

The house has gone generally green over the years. The living room is emerald in its walls, a velveteen, irridescent wallpaper bought from a decorator's service rather than Sears. The paper seems more a wish than a statement: Let there be peace in this house after the years of clutter and noise. The green is, of course, appropriate to us; as appropriate, I thought, as Jimmy's swoon.

I was thirty-four years old that summer, twice Jimmy's age and honest enough to have told him that I had no right to be there, other than the fact that I remembered him well as a child and had a continuing interest in him, again like one of those uncles. We had gone right upstairs from the living room, not ten minutes after I arrived from the airport, and there was something in the solemnity of walking up the stairs with my parents that brought a wake to mind. When I said what I said to Jim, it seemed to take a weight of embarrassment from my parents. They felt badly about my being summoned there from Japan; and my statement had a properly detached sense of brutal self-examination, enough to perhaps convince them that I had wished to come there. Which I had.

My sisters, however, the two who were there, continued to keen in the hallway. I thought to myself that they imagined it a great disgrace, not only that their youngest brother had occupied the family bathroom for three days and four nights, but also (I suspected) that the family did not have a half-bath to tide them over this crisis.

Moira and Colleen would think that; they belong to a religious cult that worships blenders and half-baths. Sally, the sensible and bawdy sister, whose husband is the great owl who painted the house's prow, I was certain would not think that way. However, I was unable to poll her then, since she had gone out with the Buddha and the Chief, my other two brothers. They had been watching the Mets game on cable TV, but left for MacDonald's to use the restrooms, since the Mets were ahead by seven runs and the game had turned uninteresting.

To my eyes, however, sitting in the greenness with generations of jet-lag pressing against my shoulders and neck in a grim, familiar force, and with only the video to tell me any-

thing—the television having been turned down but not off—
the game had a certain choreographic grace to it. In the
silence a grey uniformed shortstop received the ball deep in
the hole, where it had emerged—straight and true as a white
marble—from the fast plastic grass of the infield. The whole
process had seemed a dance of ghosts to me in those ten
minutes of rest; the infield was like a sample swatch of the
wallpaper of the room. My father explained what he called
"the situation" in a low murmur; I thought I saw geese circling
the outfield, mist rising from the slope of the pitcher's mound.

It is supposed among my family that I will think such things.
It is my eldest son's status to think them, and also, they suppose, my avocation, my true vocation. As has become clear,
each of us brothers has a nickname, and mine is suited to me as
the others are suited to them. They call me the Balding Professor, by virtue of my status as a Professor of English-as-a-
Second-Language in the institute where I teach. I would like
to say that the descriptive adjective results from what my
family thinks is my Buddhist status (they think me one; I am
not), but the truth is a Doyle genetic characteristic, a pattern
baldness. Jimmy, we call the Prince.

"Look, Jim," I said to him, after the disavowal, "It is only
anxiety you are feeling. We've all gone through it. Pat and
Brendan, and me first of all. Even Dad's had it!"

My father nodded, getting into the spirit of it. Downstairs
he had explained that it was Black Peggy, Jimmy's girl, who
was really to blame, that Jimmy missed her too much.

"It is," I said to Jim, "the curse of the Doyles. Like sickle-cell
anemia, or baldness."

The Prince laughed. Snorted really. Always a sucker for
bald jokes. It was he who gave me my name.

"Really," I said, trying to inject seriousness. He laughed
harder.

"You have him now," my father whispered.

"Come out of there, you son of a bitch," my mother said,
"I'll kill you."

"Your pupils cannot have disappeared," I said, establishing

20

a detachment again. "It is physiologically impossible for the pupils to drift from the eyeball surface. Pupils do not disappear."

There was silence. My father nodded, as much I fear from his pain—he shouldn't stay on his feet so long—as from encouragement.

"Except mine," I said, unable to resist, "my pupils always disappear in about the sixth week of classes."

The Prince laughed too loud for our comfort, then began to make a gagging sound. This was followed by the hollow, steely thump that a body makes hitting a bathtub.

My sister Colleen, as is her wont, began to scream. Always hysterical, she's a retired, trained psychologist, a year younger than me.

"He's choking to death!" she shouted. "He's choking. Batter down the door!"

Jim choked in another deep breath, still laughing.

"Batter down the door?" he said. "Who says things like batter down the door?"

I began to laugh. My mother went to her bedroom, slamming the door behind her. It made a sound like a man having his breath knocked out of him. My father made a face like he was that man.

"Mine did," my youngest brother whispered to me, "mine did disappear. They became small as pencil points, and then they just went away, like somebody erased them. And now . . ."

He waited several beats to conclude the sentence. My sister Moira sucked in her breath in a wheeze, ready to cry. Moira always loves a tragedy, whether on videotape or in real-life locked rooms. This is fortunate, because her life is sad, sadder even than Yasodhara, the wife whom the Buddha left; for her life is filled with trials and illness, and even her children are sickly. Colleen caught Moira's sadness and clung to her.

Jimmy, unerringly sensing that his audience was prepared, repeated what he had told the family during the days before I got there. "And now," he said, "I cannot move. I'm paralyzed."

Moira wept on cue, and Colleen soothed her in a professional tone. I leaped into this gap of comparative silence.

"Well then, let them come in," I said. "We can take the door from its hinges, or call the firemen if you really want a show."

"No," my father said.

"You see," the Prince said, "they think I'm a scandal."

"You sort of are," I said.

"Let me die in peace," he countered.

"I'll be long dead by then," I said, "but you do have my permission, though it's hardly Doyle-like to do anything in peace."

"If you're so damned worried about it," Jimmy said, "explain it to me. Make some sense of this. Tell me how to walk out with dignity after a week."

"It's only been five goddamned days," my father said. He was getting riled again. I'd blown it.

"Okay," I said, "I'll go downstairs and start writing it out. I'll talk to you if you come out."

"Make it good," Jimmy called out.

"I'll make what I can make," I said.

I started down the stairs.

"It's my last request," he called again.

Moira started up again as I headed down the stairs. I thought I could hear the Prince's laughter echoing hollowly from the tub.

Jimmy has always had a wonderfully accurate imagination. It *was* like a wake, with me flying in after my father's call, and DeeDee (she prefers to be called Deidre now) on her way by bus from Cambridge. In fact, one solution to the problem— which I nearly suggested then—would have been for him to play it out like Huck Finn at his own funeral. We might have made it a joke and laughed at it over dinner, the whole clan: what a trickster the Prince was, and so on.

Both he and my mother, however, would have rejected any plan like that. Jimmy wanted dignity and my mother wanted justice—or rather revenge, her peculiarly ancient notion of justice. The fact that they each would have voted against the proposition was no coincidence; they are really rather alike, dignity and revenge. They both feel too much. My father also feels too much, but he has done away with all feeling through the disciplined emptiness of patience. He is the real Buddhist. When people ask me (some do) how I came to learn to speak Japanese, I tell them truly I learned it from my father.

A wake is a Buddhist festival, patience given the form of a festival; it is a way to deflate an excess of feeling, like the slow leak of a tack in the meat of an overfilled tire. In a sense the history of Irish-American families may be said to be the history of the wake as a viable form of social ritual. Some Irish live it eternally; my brother Pat, the Chief, dreads phone calls after eleven at night; Brendan, the Buddha, says that when the phone rings at night, Pat reaches for his pin-striped suit. And yet the very word, "wake," has, as Irish literature supports, a built-in paradox, that being its sense of resurrection. My mother used to tell us we would wake the dead with our noise; in fact illustrating a dualism in the term itself. While wake is commonly taken to refer to the mourners, who in fact used to stay up several days drinking and eating and awaiting the Holy Name Society and the thunder of their baritone rosary recitation; it seems also to disclose a traditional folk belief in the efficacy of ritual as assurance at least of everlasting life. More likely, to my mind, in the Celtic fog of pre-christian history there may have been an actual tradition of physical resurrection.

My uncle Joe, Irish on my mother's side, once clearly established an empirical basis for this belief. At the wake of a hunchback fellow fireman, they cut away all but the last few strands of the undertaker's hemp-rope which held the deceased down, doing so during the afternoon when the women withdrew to cook, and the men and children were not yet home from work and school, and there were only the firemen left with the leisure and dignity to wake old Billy Hump. Later in the evening they returned, the whole squadron of them in full-dress uniform and polished buttons, waiting for the last strands to break. My uncle Joe used to have to stop when he got to this part of the story because he laughed so hard. Grown men, he would say, leaped out the window while the women shouted hallelujah.

We Irish can see the kindness. One last joke for Billy O'Hump. Or the way, when they were lowering my uncle Pat into the ground, my father's closest brother, I saw his friend Pat Lynch walk up to the lip of the grave, his hat and grey gloves in one hand. He patted the bronze side of the casket, once and once more, with his bony red hand, saying goodbye. When my father goes, I want to remember that gesture, smell the brass in the oil of my fingers.

Even in Jimmy's swoon, there was an incredible kind of lost and precise gentleness in the family's reaction. After the first night, when the family did in fact wake with Jimmy, life returned awhile to a semi-normal state. The portable toilet was brought from the camper out back and ensconced on the back porch enclosure for during the night and emergencies. Family members decided (admittedly through disgust and boredom, but ratified by Colleen's psychological lore, and a deeper historical sense) to ignore him for awhile. They brought him his letters from Black Peggy, and left food regularly, even spoke to him ("Hello, Jim, how are you?" "Disappearing still." "Fine.") when by instinct or forgetfulness they would find themselves upstairs and outside his door.

There was none of your British "Bedlam," none of the fine, civilized coercion that masks as mental health. Instead came a tenderness, a sort of *mysterium tremens*, the awe brought forth by a lost mind. Our brother the Iroquois shaman had had a vision, and we looked to see it ourselves. It is more a paradox than a proof of either our folly or modernity's wisdom that the sympathy shaded to pathos and Black Peggy came to be blamed for what was debilitating Jim.

The paradox had its root in the nature of the family mind: for she was outside it then, outside of the family, and so she was there to be blamed. A similar phenomenon had struck a few years before when Brendan went crazy just after he had met Bella (it is a Doyle trait to go crazy in the first flush of love).

Brendan is a big, handsome man, three hundred pounds of him on size eight and a half B feet, and he can dance like a chimpanzee begging bananas in the zoo. He can also sing, make whole suits of clothes, bend iron bars, outrun thin men, bake bread, waltz my mother, and paint with the eye of a lost bastard of Botticelli; besides which he eats his suppers all swirled in one big lump on his plate, potatoes, beef, lettuce and sliced peaches, while drinking water by the quart. In short, he is a renaissance man. Like any renaissance man he is caught in the serpent swirl of his own passion—because he can do so much, he (another!) feels too much. A timid giant, full of anger at himself and every wind that ever ruffled a flower, he fell in love in an angry clump, like a slumbering bull, and he woke up angrier than ever. This was complicated by the fact that none of us liked Bella, mostly because we all like Brendan so much and we wanted him to have a woman like my mother; but also because Bella *was* grand and strong like my mother. Another paradox I know, but that's how it goes. Also Bella has huge breasts, which Brendan cackled about until he made us sick.

We are all crazy, we've never been under any illusion about that. But Brendan's madness, when it came, was if anything worse than Jim's. Brendan was a danger to one and all. After nineteen years of winding that big and tensile sexual spring of his, he let loose with a passion that threatened to cut things in half. He knocked Jim unconscious with a brotherly slap at the punchline of a joke; he smashed up my father's car two days running; he wept whole nights through and loud enough that the floorboards shook under him until they were (god's truth here) audible in the kitchen below. Besides he knocked down a wall, or a portion of one, angry at him or her or both of them during a late night in which they broke up, reconciled, and broke up, twice again, in a series of phone calls. Brendan is like a dynamo: the huge running parts have a routine grace, but the smaller pistons and bushings have little tolerance. He is called Buddha because of his visage, but also I think because, like the Bodhisattva Fugen who is found on an elephant that represents love, he must endure so much complication.

Most of the already mentioned exploits of Brendan I know by other's accounts, but I personally was present for dinner during that time when he came down in the middle of the meal, still half-asleep and violently angry, and every single one of us, except my father, was in literal, mortal fear. He asked (no, demanded) that I pass the fried potatoes, and his stare made my stomach turn with fear. I had never seen such unleashed hatred, nor never will. He scraped the whole bowl of potatoes onto his plate and ate them snorting, then asked for the sausages.

The Prince said, "No need to leave the plate this time, Brendan, it's our old china."

The plate stopped in mid-air, at the end of the Buddha's long and beefy arm. The most of us held our breath as the Prince started laughing mischievously. (He may have known something; the Buddha fears only two things, bees and a phantom motorcycle gang he dreams of and who he's sure will one day come and get him. The Prince had attacked like a bee.)

"I'll kick your ass, you little shit, and use what's left to wipe up the plate."

"Brendan," my mother said. I'm not really sure whether she was afraid during those days, but I count her among the terrified if only because I have a personal intuition that she thought one day he'd strike her and she'd have to murder him.

My father was bent over his plate, studying one of two rubbery fried eggs he had just slid from a plate of them. My father generally studies his food while he eats—I think he meditates—and pauses only when it's safe to make a joke, or when he stubbornly wants to change a subject, a habit of his which my mother hates and which he claims innocence of (I think he is innocent; I'm sure he really never pays attention to what we say).

This time, however, he looked directly at Brendan.

"To touch him," he said, "you'll have to pass me, and bum legs and all I'll beat you within an inch of your life."

Now my father is not a violent man. He makes no threats other than the ones fathers make to children. The only story I ever remember about any violence in him has no violence and only a few details. A black man had gone crazy at the open hearth; he was swinging a shovel, threatening to kill anyone who came near him; my father was the foreman; he walked up and took the shovel, then bought the man coffee before sending him home on three days suspension. I was young enough when I heard the story that I still think of it in connection with John Henry, but too young to remember who told it, or how it came up. I do remember my father saying, again tenderly, "Aaron gets crazy when he drinks and his wife makes it worse." I remember the black man's name, Aaron.

So the violence of my father's response to Brendan was shocking, but it was made even worse because we had, each of us, and especially Brendan, begun the same process of forgetting my father that is going on even now. It was almost as if, when he retired with the disability of his legs and back, our father had moved out and a man who looked like him had come to board with us. Of course, he let us think that way. But within limits; Brendan had moved beyond them.

The plate of sausages hovered at the end of the big arm. Brendan's eyes stared, vile with hatred, at my father. My father stared right back, without expression.

"It is my house," my father said.

The plate dropped from the end of the arm, cracking neatly in two with a musical little click. The sausages rolled into the crevice between the two halves of the plate. Brendan burst into wheezing sobs and went from the table. We heard the front door slam and Brendan scream once, so loud it echoed through the neighborhood. Later we found out that he had run three miles in his bare feet, weeping all the while.

When he returned home, my father came into the front hall as he came in the door. Brendan didn't look at him. He began to quiver like a huge bird, and the sobs came again.

"Oh grow up, you big ox," my father said.

"I'm sorry," Brendan whispered.

"I saved you a sausage," my father said.

The point is this all passed. Bella proved herself by not trying to prove herself, or by proving to Brendan. She began to sit in the kitchen and talk to my mother, and by this process entered into the stories. For, among us Doyles, entering into the stories is perhaps more important than birth; it is where you get your personality, and where you can get it back; where your qualities, moods, and indeed your private speech is determined, and where you must act in order to change any of them. And my mother, as keeper of the kitchen table, the porch, and other gathering places, is keeper of the stories. In this way only it is fair to say that she started up the resentment about both Bella and Black Peggy, for they had no stories, no interlocking surfaces.

Sardonic, moody, witty, and bitter, my mother is a leviathan, a genuinely huge and I think beautiful woman, a witch, a Scheherazade of stories; she keeps things straight, or bends them to suit her, and looks out for her children and family, especially the males, who she understands are weak and need her help. If love is a heart transplant, my mother is the Doyle antibody and immunosuppressant in one substance. She seeks out and isolates the new heart, then as quickly teaches it the knobs and whirls of the Doyle genetic code. Perhaps this is because she herself is an unwilling transplant; unwilling, and largely unwilled (as any of our women). My father had three brothers and four sons, the script is the same: Doyles marry for continuity, taking on leading ladies and treating them like additions to the audience who've wandered on the stage for a closer look. I too did this.

And Jimmy also, I imagine. The problem was that Black Peggy sought a private performance; she of all our women seemed nearest to my mother in this one thing. Thus Peggy was not around enough to grow stories, and that is where the trouble started. This time, however, my father was home for good and not for the sixteen hours that came between shifts, and he, curious to say, did not understand the biology, the immunology. He thought when my mother hated Black Peggy that she really did. (She really did.) He did not understand—and this is even more curious to say—that my mother rejects every implantation because that is how she learned to protect him and us. She is an anarchist, a terrorist in the old and comfortable working class sense of Sacco and Vanzetti or the Mad Bomber. Yet she is also a Buddhist in that she rejects all as illusion; she gives nothing love that is not capable of giving nothing but love. Strong words, I know, even adoring words; but how else explain the vehemence of her rejection of all things and people?

When my father retired, my mother said this to me, "He was always such a strong man and now he's wasting away." No mother has the right to share such ferocity with a son; no mother, that is, but one who sees the ferocity in this exploiting world.

When Siddhartha Gautama was born, the court astrologer divined from his birthmarks that he would become a Buddha. The astrologer said the boy would see Four Visions, an ancient man, a sick man, a dead man, and a holy man. Suddhodana, the father, said, "Let such sights be forbidden in the palace."

I think the story means that Suddhodana did not understand that his son would someday see him. That is, the story is essentially the same one as the riddle of the Sphinx. Suddhodana's order was unenforceable, as events made clear.

Here is another of the stories:

I could not have been more than four years old. There was a strike at the plant, and my father was a union man then, as he was all the time until I went into the sixth grade and he became a foreman, and soon after we came to this house.

The strike this time had continued for many months, beginning in early autumn and extending through the grey beginnings of winter, already up to the last few weeks before Christmas. It could have been bad for us; by then there were Colleen and Sally in the family. There was no money, no strike fund, and already there were five of us.

My father, however, was quite a remarkable man, a photographer, and he had been able to pick up a few weddings to photograph. The fees for these provided enough.

"Butter and coal," he said.

Sometimes my mother would help him, tinting the cameo enlargements; these were very profitable items and popular then. The photographic tints were difficult to handle, oily pigments; but my mother brought uniformity and light to the flesh tones and painted the eyes and mouths with the delicacy of watercolor. Some of these prints are still very beautiful to look at; there is a pair of facing portraits which she tinted, of my father and her, which sit now on the piano in the front hall. I look like he does in this portrait.

With the coming of winter, there had been no weddings for several weeks and money was getting short. We kids could not help but hear. One night my mother was crying alone at the table and could not say why.

My father devised a plan. They had taken a picture of me dressed in my snowsuit; it actually is a very funny picture: the small, brimmed hat over the cherubic face, the tight leggings looped under rubber boots, which I recall—although the pictures were not in color—were red.

My mother had made a snow scene out of cotton and soap flakes. It was to be the background: one round snowman to the right of a drift of soapflake snow, and, on the left, a reindeer, which was actually made of wax, a seasonal candle. They made a composite of the picture of me in the snowsuit against this background, to be used as a Christmas card: a happy, waving, fat-faced boy midst the cotton snowman, the waxen reindeer, drifts of soapflake snow.

It was my father's idea to sell cards door-to-door, using this card as a sample, offering people their own personalized Christmas cards, with their children frolicking in this winter scene. It was really an ambitious scheme since the cards were difficult to make, involving as they did the different composites and enlargements, the processing and packaging.

The day I remember was bitter with cold and driving, slushy hail, small crystals snapping against the windows and coating the sidewalks with a crunched glaze. My father was preparing to go out to sell the cards. He was packing the olive drab shoulder-strap canvas bag he used for equipment. Army surplus, the bag was compartmented inside, several irregularly shaped sections that had been used for storing things. I asked him what things.

"Ammunition or medicine. Yes . . . medicine."

First he packed several of the black metal film plates, stuffing them into a rubberized inner pocket. Then a number of packets of flash bulbs, each packet corrugated cardboard, fine silver hairs of filament inside the bulbs.

Finally he packed a great many samples of the card with my picture; on the back of each he had printed by hand the price per ten cards, our address and phone, and his name. Also thrown on top of the bag was a box of business cards he had printed long before, each one imprinted with this line: "Expert in wedding albums . . . Inquire about our Custom Tinting of Your Prints or Old Photographs."

He wore a heavy tweed coat with padded shoulders, it reached to the middle of his shins. Around his neck was a plaid scarf, wool, beneath which one of my mother's sweaters peeked through from under the overcoat. He always wore a brimmed hat then, with a peak like a baseball cap or a duck's bill, the inner flaps folded down over his ears. He smiled. His face was flushed from all the clothes and the heat in the hallway.

Last to go in the bag was a large press camera, its lens retracted and the flap folded up and locked. The shallow flash pan was detached and placed in a pocket; the camera set atop everything. Then he closed the inner rubber flaps of the canvas bag, and strapped it closed.

He kissed us goodbye and went out into the snow.

It is amusing to think of the many unknown people who perhaps retain my picture, somewhere in large cardboard boxes: the snowsuit, the glee hand, the smile, the celebratory reindeer.

rituals
and customs

At the age of twenty-nine, I confessed to my mother that I
had been in the presence of a woman's flesh long before I had
been in the presence of blood rare roast beef. She seemed
doubly shocked by this remark, but also I think doubly
amused. Amused first because I have long suspected she is
amused by cooking badly (although leathery roast beef is an
Irish custom), since really she hates cooking at all. Second,
because I have long known, and Pat for one has exploited as a
lifestyle with her, her affection for bawdy. For instance, when
I first introduced Mary to her, I was making a cup of tea for
Mary and stumbled just as I set it down on the table. The
boiling spillage ended in the lap of Mary's skirt. She leaped up
and shouted.

"Goddamn it, Edmund, my thighs are burning, you clumsy
oaf."

My mother never looked up.

"But that's why you're marrying him, isn't it?" she asked.

Mary entered into the stories immediately when she smiled and said, "Yes, but I don't expect him to be clumsy about it."

I mention the subject of beef and women because I had convinced myself that Jimmy's crisis was the sort of ritual occasion which would signal roast beef on the table. I was wrong. No one wanted to cook, or more accurately everyone wanted to have what they quaintly call "take outs."

So we sent for chicken wings, which in Buffalo have metamorphosized into fiery little stubs of gristle and meat which are bathed in red hot sauce and then, before eating, drowned in little plastic tubs of bleu cheese dressing. Scrubbed wands of celery are also included with each order, either as a gesture toward the concept of a balanced meal, or, more likely, as a cheap way to swallow the last puddle of the bleu cheese with some dignity.

The city of Buffalo has more taverns than Elizabeth's Irish England, and every tavern serves food (be it so humble as a jug of cooked eggs in vinegar, pickled embryo), thus making the city the bar-food capital of Christianity. The reasons for this are manifold, having to do historically with the ethnicity of the city, sociologically with its decentralization and the role of the tavern as a surrogate home. Philosophically, however, the prevalence of food is, I think, rooted in the rootlessness, the clarified existential ennui of the city's character, its outskirtsness. It is literally impossible to walk two blocks of a commercial street without coming upon a food shop, whether a bar or the hundreds of storefront take-out places (it is the same in Tokyo, but the noodle shops have so many more people to nourish). Buffalonians are, I think, similar in nature to their totemic namesakes; they are grazing animals, creatures of instants, and this attention to instants makes the city archetypically working class. For no one cares about anything.

I cannot put it more clearly. In the period of historical time that encompassed Jimmy's swoon, the unemployment rate in the city was an official twelve percent, with actual estimates ranging toward twenty percent (taking into account the workless who have exhausted their benefits and therefore no longer statistically exist, having "left the working force," you'll find them eating clams or ribs at the take-out bars). And yet a stranger, say someone from our district in Japan, touring the city, would never fathom the fact. Unless of course he could lay in the sour space between a husband and wife at night after the bars have closed.

Which is to say, one grows up into the momentariness in my city. So too, once the Buddha and the Prince had reached their adolescence and my mother could argue both the lack of presence of growing children and the lack of acceptable menu choices to suit their sapling appetites, take-outs became a regular occurence at the family table. Hot dogs, submarines, wings, beef on weck (the German kummelweck or cumin-seed roll, peculiar to Buffalo), fried fish, tacos, steak sandwiches with sauteed dandelion green; all found their time and place. That day it was wings; and they seemed appropriate both temporally (as they suggested passing time and flight) and spatially (again as they suggested flight, specifically Jimmy's from reality).

The last comments were Pat's, who stayed for dinner that night, along with his Renoiresque and giddy wife, Miranda. It was good to have them there, for we were otherwise reduced in number, with Colleen gone home to Fred and their daughter; Moira gone home to television and her sadnesses; DeeDee still on the bus about to start the long drop down from Albany and homeward; and, finally, Bella having to work. Jimmy, of course, remained in his tile mausoleum, without center to his vision, but with a take-out box of wings going cold outside his door, the sacrificial offering of a meal having become a custom among them.

Pat's attendance was crucial to me, first because I am closest to him (kinship bonds pass chronologically in our family, but according to gender: Pat and I are close, also Brendan and Jimmy and Colleen and Sally; Moira is alone with her intricate woe, and Deidre with her intricate and distant intelligence, thus proving exceptions). But also Pat and Miranda added substance enough to the sum present so as to activate the family mind.

Because it takes five or more to enact a family mind, I am convinced first that the most of America (and Japan for that matter) will never again experience it; and convinced second that the source of much of Brendan's and Jimmy's excessive vulnerability proceeds from the more or less general desertion of the family mind from their day-to-day lives.

For in the family mind everyone is freed unto meaninglessness, becoming part of a general babble; without it, each one is thrown back on the shell of self more than is healthy (given, that is, the omnipresent need for the shell in the world of snails beyond the door). Five at the table means there's always an odd one out; someone able to provide running commentary, tangential madness, worry, bother, or delirium. Five or more also means a potential for synapsis, for a mad or random linkage making more sense than any one burdened intelligence could have generated on its own. More, the synapsis is immediate, outside of logic, and therefore never has to be spoken: we all talk and talk and joke and joke and somehow, years or days later, realize what we've realized, and know it so well there's no need to tell anyone.

In this way, the family mind is similar or identical to the stories; but in another way also. Take Pat's remark. It is what is expected of him, since he is generally labelled "a brooder" in the stories, and therefore he can suggest a level of external truth that from any of the other of us would seem heretical. It was alright, for instance, for me to agree with Jimmy that they thought him a scandal—even to suggest it myself; for I am understood to be the one concerned with "rightness." Even my occupation ratifies that for the family mind and the stories: I think they think me in actual charge of the language, when as a matter of fact I am heartened and amused when my students mangle and poeticize it. However, for me to suggest that about myself, or worse, to do as Pat, and say that Jimmy had fled reality on clipped but fiery wings, would be seen as cruel. For I would be abusing my right to the rightness, turning it against Jimmy.

The same of course holds for Brendan, who is expected

to be large and excessive, and Sally to be naughty, and so on up (my father watches his wings, as if they might flee on him) and down the line (they awaited Deidre like a judgement, she would know what the WASPs would think, but ironically wouldn't care; capable of spending her whole weekend home without noticing that Jimmy was *en cabinet* at all; her bus crept toward Syracuse, you could see the map unwind in my father's eyes, when now and then he looked up. The fact was that if Greyhound travelled neighborhood streets, he would have arisen and walked to the door the instant it turned our corner).

Here then is the extreme irony and awe. For the family mind, that soup, depends on the individuality of each present; so much so that it functions paradoxically. What would seem on the surface an extreme loss of definition, is, in fact, a continual and simultaneous process of definition. This was what the Buddha and the Prince had lost and grieved for.

This, too, was what I longed for, and the number around the table supplied. For everyone was worried, despite the outward calm. If we were a family of East Indians, each would have had a blood red jewel in the forehead to signify worry. Instead we calmly ate our chicken like the Gautama did, when he ate the curried hen that Sujata brought him, before he sat under the Bo tree and Mara assailed him.

Harry, the owl husband of Sally, raised his eyebrows into arcs when Pat made his remark. Their son Sean wandered in and out of the dining room and onto the back porch, delighted to have a toilet there. The family mind went on, far from Pat's homily regarding flight.

Harry spoke. "Too bad they don't sell wild game takeout giblets," he said, "then Jimmy's flight would be the right brother's at kidney hawk."

My mother groaned; the family mind groaned. Harry enters the stories as someone who likes to plot out elaborate bad jokes then offer them dryly, delighted with groans. He grinned broadly, broader still when Sally replied, "Jezus, Harry, you've got a sense of humor as small as a hawk's balls."

"Sally!" my mother exclaimed, trying not to laugh.

Suddenly there was a brief flurry of optimistic excitement, for my father returned from upstairs with news that Jim had eaten his wings. All of us rose up, except Buddha and my mother. My mother remained seated because she wanted to embarrass my father with the truth before she showed any hope.

"What'd you go up there to check on him?" she asked.

"No," my father lied, "I forgot about him. I was going to the john . . ."

"Well, why don't you go?" she called him.

By this time, those of us who were standing were impatient to do something. What I don't know, unless examine the relics, the empty tomb.

"Next let's leave him a bottle of coke," Miranda said. "We'll put it under one of those boxes with a stick and string, then trap him when he comes out."

She began to giggle.

"Wait," the Buddha said.

He was still sitting because he had eaten the wings, a fact he admitted sheepishly, quenching the fires of hope.

"I was making a phone call," he said, "and I got hungry."

It was shameful that he did so, not because the Prince needed the sustenance—my mother claimed he had provisioned himself, and I suspected she was right, we Doyle's come prepared, even for psychosis—but because, before he went to make his call, Brendan had just consumed some three dozen of the wings.

"Everything in excess," has long been a Doyle motto, especially for occasions involving food and drink. Chicken wings are bipartite: a fat little thigh like a shrunken drumstick, and a pointed piece of gristly twin bones whose only meat is a recognizable strand of ligament or whatever between the shafts. The wings are sold by the dozen, with a dozen computed by the number of shafts and thighs. They are packaged in the same pristine white cardboard boxes as carnations. The secret of eating them, at least among us, is to grab as many of the thighs as possible and avoid starvation. The Chief and the

Buddha accomplish this by inhaling the meat while the rest of us tarry chewing. They exhale tiny bones between each dwarfed drumstick and stack the white boxes before them to form a wall. The Buddha seemed now to crouch down behind the wall.

Those of us who had been standing pending the miracle, sat down after Brendan's revelation.

"For Christ's sake, Brendan, Jimmy's sick," my mother said.

"Deidre's outside of Rochester," my father announced.

Sally's Sean wandered in from the porch again, this time holding the gallon jug of chemicals for the portable toilet. The blue moustache on his face suggested that he'd drunk from the jug.

Harry jumped up. "Excuse us," he said, "we'd better get going to the hospital."

Sally handed Sean to his father; Sean screamed for dessert.

"Do you think we should ask Jimmy if he wants to go too?" Sally asked. "If he went to the emergency room now, it would save an extra trip . . ." She cackled (always in the stories this is Sally's euphemism; she cackles says my mother, and actually she does). One is never sure how serious Sally is at these times.

"No, no, go . . ." my mother said, but Sally already had.

The Buddha began to weep, the pains of children trouble him.

"Damn that Black Irish Peggy," my father said.

My mother turned on him, snapping. "Don't be ignorant, Matt," she said. It was her way of worrying about Sean, to turn on my father; who, in his own way, was worrying about Sean under the guise of worrying about Jim. What's more, my father was merely quoting my mother who had used the same phrase at the beginning of dinner. "They'll pump his stomach," said Pat the Chief, who concerns himself with physical details as well as mental. "Stop slobbering, Brendan," my father said, striking back at my mother. "Maybe they should have taken the chemical jug to show the doctors," said Miranda, who also thinks about physical details, but with more common sense than Pat, because she works in a hospital. Then she went into the kitchen for coffee, since the mood had turned ugly, my mother's storms blackening everyone. The phone rang and Pat stood, but Brendan shouted, "I've got it!" The shout at the ring of a phone is a family custom, and usually takes precedence over physical proximity to the instrument. The phone rang twice more.

"Well, get it, damn it!" my mother said.

But Pat already had, having snuck around the long way, through the kitchen, while Brendan started on the direct route through the living room. We all quieted to hear the conversation.

"Yes, I'll get it," Pat said, "but did they put a hose down his throat or what?"

It was Sally, calling from the hospital about the ingredients in the chemicals. Sean was fine, his stomach had already been pumped. The hospital is only minutes away; we use it often.

"The little blighter," my mother said, meaning Sean. She laughed then, the storm dissipating.

"It looked like a face full of grapes," Miranda said, laughing with my mother.

A story about Sean was appended to the story of the Prince's swoon.

"He's still only a kid," my father said.

We all knew he meant Jimmy.

"Yes," my mother said, "but he's afraid of something."

"Anybody'd fear vanishing in this house," the Chief said. "Sean could be dead. They told him the tube was like an astronaut."

Miranda served coffee. There was a breeze through the house, a cool woodland wind, the special breath of summer. It had somehow found its way through the narrow streets, the convergence of grey houses, dark trees, automobiles, and crickets; a breeze like someone had rolled the stone from the top of a cool, dry well of Indian air. It had found its way into the house, through all the darkening rooms, spreading among us as we drank our sweet, strong coffee. People were silent, meditating the simple taste of the coffee. Brendan hummed a song as the family mind moved on. Jimmy was resting in the cool of the tub, a moist washcloth across his eyes like a balm of rose petals. I knew somehow that what had been decided was that Jimmy should be given understanding, that we should leave room for him to come back into, that everyone deserved the dignity of an escape. I knew also that my father was already plotting revenge on Black Peggy for the trouble she caused my mother. You could feet it in his silence; it was understood in the family mind. There was nothing I could do, nothing anyone could have done, although I think now I should have done something instead of drinking my coffee, feeling the breeze. But the jet lag had slipped up on me again, catching me in its yawning; people were talking quietly now, Pat wanted to know about the Black Irish and so they talked about that. I excused myself and went to bed, going all the way up to the third floor, the room carved out of the attic. It was silent there, more silent than it ever is in Japan. The house breathes upward, the third floor was full of thick, silent air, the hot exhalation of the house, and only a thin rope of the breeze wound its way upward. I lay down in the silence, the thick air around me, and above me on the roof the cottonwood tufts lay down their seeds, one atop the other, in an insulating cushion. I dreamed that a forest of cottonwood grew from the roof, thousands of saplings swaying in a wave with the summer breeze.

Two people woke me during that night. The first was Pat, he had climbed the stairs like a hill just before he and Miranda left. He sat puffing and sweating in the swivel chair at the old desk; I could hear his puffing, smell the sweet, vulnerable scent that is the Chief's when he perspires. We had shared a room for years.

I woke in a jolt and heard him, smelled him, there.

"Can you wake up for awhile?"

"I don't know. What time is it?"

"Sean came back before they went home. He wanted his dessert."

"Get me a cigarette, they're in my pants, next to the desk."

The Chief probed along the floor for the pants as he talked.

"Then he wanted to go back to the hospital to have them pump it out." He threw the pack up on the bed. "What do you think?" he asked.

"I need a light. A match."

He threw me the matches, I lit a cigarette and sat up against the bedstead.

"It must be four in the morning," I said.

"Two. Well?"

"What?" I asked. "You mean about Jimmy. Or about them?"

"What do you know about Black Irish?"

"Sy's one," I said.

Sy is my father's youngest brother. He is a foot doctor, like my Uncle Pat was. Sy was the Prince in my father's family.

"I know," Pat said, "but tell me what it means."

"What'd they say downstairs?"

"I want to hear from you."

"You'd be Black Irish if you were darker. Because of your charm, and your brooding. It's mostly physical, the hair and eyes and fair skin, but they have attributes. Maybe because of their looks . . ."

"The looks bring them?" Pat asked. "You mean like an omen?"

"With the Irish it can be either way. It could just as well be the other way around. Maybe they develop the attributes because of the looks. You never know."

"Moira's one."

"Yes, Moira's one. It's that kind of plump baby quality, with a little of the Indian Princess thrown in."

When she was younger, very young, we convinced Moira that she was adopted, that she had been an Indian. She added the Princess to it. Moira was the baby of the older family, we five. Seven years lapsed between Moira and Deidre, and the youngest three constitute their own clan. I don't know who started the Indian story—it may have been my mother—but we all played along with it.

42

Sitting there in the dark, listening to Pat's puffing breath, it seemed that we might have perpetrated the story exactly because she was Black Irish. To single her out among us as she was singled out by birth; her black gypsy beauty, the raven hair and brown eyes, one eye mysteriously furled from birth as the result of a myosis. Even after the eye was operated on, the lid remained hooded, partially dimmed, like the outer petals of a rosebud. It made her look remote and beautiful. The Irish as a race are not beautiful, but the Black Irish are. Perhaps that is why they are given attributes, why they are known for actors and priests. Moira's attributes are patience with children beyond human tolerance, illnesses and palenesses, innocence, story telling, and, of course, the ability to live with pain.

One of Moira's children is dying and a friend of Pat's is a doctor at the Children's Hospital. The friend took Moira out for coffee once, and when Pat called him afterward, the doctor—who is not Irish—said, "She is either very stupid, or a brave idealist." None of us is stupid. It is just that Moira tells stories, and she does not spare herself them. Some people see this as idealism. Moira however does more than tell stories, she lies, sometimes beautifully. This and beauty make her faintly dangerous. She said a man stopped her once on a New York street and offered her a modelling contract. With anyone else, I would think the tale was either a lie or the history of an encounter with a pornographer. I believe this story of Moira's. She was taking her son to a specialist there, and she could not stay in the city. She might have been rich. She might have been known as the Indian beauty of Bloomingdale's ads. For I think she still believes our story.

My uncle Sy's attributes are parsimony and wit, as well as charm with women and children. He is known to be devil-may-care, and the family story about him concerns the Second World War. Sy was drafted late and sent to Washington as a typist. The typist he replaced, a WAC, was sent to Europe, to the combat zone. Sy wears his black hair oiled back like a snake-oil salesman, and yet he is charming. He likes to wear baby-blue suits, summer and winter, and when he examines the feet of patients it is as if he were judging a beauty contest for infants. My father is not close to Sy—neither Sy's fault nor my father's—but rather the way of the youngest and oldest, princes and professors. And yet, when my uncle Pat died, Sy drank so much whiskey that he walked out to the road, down the long slope from his country house, and sat drunkenly against a cedar tree, weeping until he slept. My father would let no one else touch him. He walked down alone and gathered Sy in his arms, carrying him back to the house and putting him to bed. My father's back hurt so much that he could not get out of bed for two full days; yet he and Sy did not talk for months after that, until someone's birthday brought them together again. Then Sy's wife mentioned the funeral breakfast, how my father carried Sy. They both denied it. My father said Sy had been tired, but he had not carried him. No one contradicted them, although we all had watched from the window—aunts, cousins and children, some thirty or more of us in the large picture window.

Pat said, "You'll burn your fingers. You're dreaming."

"Thinking."

"What will they do?"

"Probably take him in to the doctor for a check-up," I said.

"No," Pat said, "that's already decided. I mean, you're right. They were talking about taking him to the emergency room when he comes out. The family line is that Jimmy had a fainting spell and then got scared, hysterical, and wouldn't come out. They said he's been run-down. They suspect the flu or mono."

"He's a truant," I said. "We all were, but the Prince has it figured."

"I mean them," Pat said.

When the Chief is particularly worried, or otherwise thinking very rigorously, the puffed breathing all moves to his nostrils. He snorts, and grunts his words, building inward pressure like a steam boiler. Pat is a boiler keeper by profession, seasonally unemployed; he works for the schools in the great civil service tradition of our people, and collects benefits for his seasonal unemployment, in the great political tradition. He is a poet mainly, in the great tradition.

I didn't know what to say; he meant my parents.

"She wants him to be young again," Pat said.

I nodded, he could not have seen me. The cigarette had burned down to the filter, and I held it between my fingers watching it burn inward like a fired stump.

"I feel like she wants us to reject him," I said, "because he is no longer who she wants him to be. Because rejecting him, like her, we will be loving him."

"I think the Prince is holding them hostage," Pat said.

"At home now we have a garden," I said. "I was thinking at dinner that I should say something about a garden here. That I'd put one in before I leave; but then I realized they wouldn't tend it. I even knew I wouldn't tend it if I was still here."

The Chief snorted, a hiss of air, like a valve blowing out.

"They have no goals," I said.

"Yes, they have no goals," the Chief repeated.

"It seems like either she won't talk to him, or else she fights him. Both ways just keeping him alive."

"The thing is he's boring," Pat said, "and now that they're together all the time, now that he's here with everybody, he can't hide it."

"Whose goddamn fault is that?" I snapped at Pat, then frisked and patted the bedclothes, hunting for another cigarette. Another valve blew, and this time he hissed air from his nostrils and mouth both in an unvoiced whistle. As I struck the match, I saw his head moving slowly back and forth as he calmed himself. I was wrong to snap at him. It was brave of him to say what he had said; it was something we all knew, something I might have said. I had felt my temper flare, and my voice took an edge like my mother's voice.

"I'm sorry," I said, my voice raspy, tired. "Between the plant and the family, he used all his time. He has no friends, no interests, except the darkroom."

"I know that!"

Beneath Pat's anger there was a whimper. I had hurt him more than I thought.

"I know," I said, "I'm explaining it to myself."

"Yeah . . ." Pat stood up, he was trying to think how to leave. "It was bad when Pat died," the Chief said.

The last time I had been home, my uncle Pat was a half-year dead. I remembered watching my father with new eyes then, seeing how lonely he was, simply that. With no one to talk to he had playacted being a sports fan to keep in step with his youngest sons. They were watching basketball on TV, my father was excited, a sixty year old cheerleader with the tone of a grizzled sportscaster. He had walked into the room midway in the third period.

"Those Braves can do it," he enthused. "They just stand there and shoot!"

"They haven't tonight, they stink," muttered one of the boys.

"Yes, they stink," my father said sadly.

"No rebounding," the other boy said.

"No, they don't rebound, but . . ." my father began again.

The boys had never looked up at him. They were both sprawled on the floor, their feet toward the tube, their heads propped up on angled elbows, each with one hand to one ear, the other ear open to the endless enthusiasm of the television commentators. My father stood at the apex of the triangle made by their bodies, standing over their heads, studying the screen, trying, I thought, to find out something to speak about that they would agree upon. Other men had learned these things through the years, I thought; other men went to have a beer and watch the game after work, and did not come home to their families. It is a choice, I thought. Still, I wanted to kick the Buddha and the Prince, to walk over and kick at their propped skulls.

"You're right, Dad," I said. "Generally, the Braves are finesse shooters. You hardly know that they're scoring."

46

"They have no rebounding," he said. "Shooting's not enough, especially when they're cold like tonight. They stink."

He had shut me off like I was stupid, it annoyed me. I found it hard to feel anything but anger, although I knew he had gained some ground by shutting me off. The boys, however, acknowledged nothing, their eyes still scanning the violet shadows of the color images. They ignored him without knowing, just as I sometimes found myself doing when he called on the phone. He would be talking on and on about something (one of my sisters or brothers, or their children, or sports, he was learning quickly about sports, applying himself to his new religion), and I would find myself reading something from a newspaper, an American-style advice column in the Tokyo daily, and I'd force myself to pay attention, only to find out that I was really bored.

My father had cut me off for defending him against what he did not want to be defended against. He had wanted to win on his own terms, with Brendan and Jimmy. He had to catch up; it was his choice. It was no choice at all actually; I knew that then. All those years of barroom conversations he had passed up for his family were no choice at all; any of the men who did go to the bars might have told you that, if they were able to say. What kind of choice is it when you have to decide between work, self, and family, any two but not three? A wage-slave's choice, a determination. I had friends whose fathers were the barroom sports fans. My friends hate their fathers, but they are able to talk to them about these things. My father could not talk about anything to the children who loved him for his presence. It's no wonder the Irish are fond of sad ballads. There is a similar lost choice in every ballad.

Pat was right about his eponymous uncle. Even the way my father had cut me off that time was like how he and his brother Pat argued. My brothers and I had made a family joke of it. "You're right," we'd say, "but that's where you're exactly wrong." My father and uncle Pat argued that way. They had nothing in common but themselves, their long knowledge of each other, and at family gatherings they would eventually end up in the kitchen, my uncle pouring three-finger shots of Canadian Club. They'd argue politics, religion, sports, western civilization. One would talk and talk, the other nodding and sipping until the first pause. "You're right," he'd say, "but that's where you're exactly wrong," and then he would talk while the other sipped.

My brother Pat was still standing; my second cigarette had burned down hot. We heard the clump-clump of my mother coming up the second-floor stairs, heard her limp down the hall, stiff with arthritis or bad veins, puffing out of breath from the climb, the click of the bedroom door.

"The only sport he ever played was soccer," I said to Pat.

"Yes, yes," he said. "He's worried about her."

"Just look how she tells something," I said, "like tonight at dinner."

We had been talking about my aunt, and my mother wondered why it was that my aunt was the same age as she and yet my aunt could do all her housework. I said, "It's because you don't like to, don't want to." She said, "But I can't walk, can't get around." It was the first we heard of this current pain, and now she limped.

"She wants us to feel bad," Pat said.

It was cruel, but exact: he meant she wanted us to feel bad about everything, Jimmy, herself, everything.

Someone else came up the stairs then, soft feet, stopping at the bottom of the third-floor stairs.

"Pat . . . Pat . . ." Miranda whispered. "Are you asleep?"

"Coming," he said aloud.

"Everyone's going to sleep," she whispered, and then retreated with the same soft steps.

"Is Deidre home?" I asked.

Pat laughed aloud.

"You'll like this. No sooner does she get in the door and sit down with a cup of tea, then Dad tells about this dream he had. Really unusual for him. One of his angelfish got out of the aquarium and it had grown this big, he said, gesturing with his arms out. It was flying around the house, and he kept trying to catch it by sticking a record under it . . .”

Pat was laughing again, a loud har-har, it was the only noise in the house.

“Deidre,” he said, “waited til he finished. It's a death dream, she said, and sipped her tea. The old man looked proud.”

In the Sanin district where we used to live, before moving to the outskirts of Tokyo, everyone farmed, and so we call it Iowa. My colleagues at the Institute make irritated jokes whenever I talk about Iowa, but I suspect they cannot help but believe my insistence that everything was better there. The rice farms were like a pond grown over in water lilies, the dark jade squares of the fields pushing against each other, and yet floating in place. Even the hogs were magnificent, blessed beasts, huge as elephants and clean pink or pink and grey. And to watch someone catch a carp was to see a rainbow on the end of a line, like the dueling kites at Hamamatsu pulling with the muscle of the wind.

But what, my colleagues tease me, makes these yokels so much better than we are? I answer that they valued each man or woman according to his or her worth, that they were essentially democratic, fair as the soil. My colleagues laugh outrageously, I think because they know I hate it here, but also because they know life is so small here, contaminated by the machines. It is beautiful country in this district, but gears are growing under the soil and the grass comes up sour. Even the gardens are interspersed with concrete creatures which the residents claim to find beautiful, but which wither the shrubs in their proximity.

People in our district consider this a political and religious center. The politics are neo-classical conservative, and it is not the emperor but the managers who are revered. The local Shinto cult is similar, not the ancient way that the name Shinto

49

commemorates, but a reactionary way; the people resent recent capitalist scandals only because they obscure what many think was a return to the right way, a sense of order. They hate outsiders, especially the dark-skinned Koreans and Thais, and everywhere you go you can hear rascist remarks, often in the same conversations that venerate the cults. Jesus called to mind to vindicate hate for the niggers. I point this out to both colleagues and students. My students have no evident dislike for me, but rather hate this place themselves, although they will all live here.

There is an annual peony festival here which combines both cult and politics; a Chamber of Commerce initiated ritual meant to establish our city as the peony city, although the blooms here are no more distinguished than anywhere else. Every year a queen is selected, in the American way, and she and her court ride in the peony parade. I have never attended the parade, or for that matter any of the festival events, but one year an event took place in the parade which I would choose to recall as my sole memory of the spirit of this place.

It was the year of the American bicentennial and one of the parade participants constructed a miniature covered wagon, which she harnessed to four huge St. Bernard dogs. It was a very popular float, especially since in recent years letters to the newspaper editor have complained that the parade has become nothing but automobiles. During the course of the parade, the dogs began to weary. It was very hot and their tongues extended like eels, and the woman had to prod them in the flanks to keep them moving. Three-quarters of the way along the route, one dog died and the woman withdrew. Two more dogs slumped beside the first dog at the roadside, and the fourth had to be rushed to a veterinary in order to save its life. I often think of those dogs, slumped at the roadside as the floats pass by, peony-sided displays crawling with unseen black ants as the queen waves.

It is, of course, unsurprising that there have been complaints about the numbers of cars in the parade. Our nearest neighbor, for instance, has three automobiles, an outboard motor, a chain saw, a lawn mower, a motorbike, and a snow-mobile, all running on gasoline. He is a manager and so can afford these things.

I was awakened the second time by a hand gagging my mouth. "Shhh . . ." Jimmy whispered, and motioned for me to follow him. There was enough light in the room to be able to see his face, but it was still dark outside, still early morning, his face appearing grey as mist in the shallow light.

He waited while I dressed and lit a cigarette, and then he started down the stairs, walking carefully but not over-cautiously since there was little fear that anyone would wake in our house. It was damply cool outside, the air of very early morning like the breeze of the previous evening. A foggy aura looped down from each of the street lights and the houses were greyer than ever. We went halfway down the block in silence.

"So, you've been going out every night," I whispered, laughing at the idea.

Jimmy stopped dead in his tracks and glared at me. He was hurt by my amusement, a glaze of hurt covered the anger in his eyes. He shook slightly, though whether from anger or the slight early morning chill I could not tell.

"No," he said sharply, and bit his lip, "Damn it, I am still disappearing. I just wanted you to see, so you'd understand when they take me out."

We stood there facing each other. I noticed lights in the Moriarity's house and the Pollak's, someone in the latter's window.

"If you want to see, come quietly," Jimmy said. "But if you just want to pick on me, you can go back to bed."

"Are we going to see Peggy?"

"No," he said disdainfully, "she's still at school. Are you coming or not?"

We walked quietly again, down around the corner and up to Seneca Street, the main thoroughfare. As we walked past the

Cazenovia Grill, I could see that there were still three men sitting at the bar drinking beer in the dark. From the way the light boiled softly in the eastern sky, I knew it had to be about five o'clock, the bars an hour past closing but still these men sat there. The streetlight at the park drive changed once without any traffic, but then two cars in a row came north, heading into Buffalo for an early shift. The birds were beginning to wake as we went into the park, still walking in silence next to each other.

Cazenovia Park is one of two parks Frederick Law Olmstead designed in Buffalo after he had finished Central Park in Manhattan. Like all his creations it has a nineteenth-century strength of concept, a functional and pragmatic beauty sculpted deep into the land, even after years of "progress" have filled his moats, drained his boating pond for baseball fields and replaced his grand central meadow with a golf course. There is a handsome stone bridge that crosses over no water in one of the places where the moats were filled before memory. This one bridge remains. It is like us all here, isolated, graceful, and hard. It is there, in that cave beneath the bridge, that Jimmy and his friends drank beer and smoked joints and dodged the constant police. There also that they brought the girls, as soon as the girls would go there. Once my parents had to pick up Jimmy at the police station. He had been caught with the boys drinking beer. Jimmy told my parents that he was only watching and talking, and they believed him. He also told them that the police had watched his friend Butch buy the beer, then waited long enough for the kids to get to the bridge before they pushed the squad car up over the curb and sailed across the lawn with the lights flashing in silence. Jimmy's suggestion was that the police hassled them to get the beer. In fact, he suggested that was why they had been taken in, because they had called the cops on the scheme. My father listened in silence and drove back to the station. He says that when he confronted the desk sergeant with Jimmy's charge, the sergeant smiled and said, "So . . ."

"So I told him he was son of a bitch," my father said.

"You're lucky you weren't arrested," my mother said.

"The son of a bitch just grinned again," my father said.

My mother had not understood about our police. My brother Pat does. Pat says that if he were driving with an open bottle of whiskey or a lid of dope, he would rather be stopped by the Buffalo police than any in the world.

"It's just that they understand," he said. "They're just working-class lugs like everyone else."

I had thought Jimmy was taking me to the bridge, but we cut south through the park instead of going across it. We passed through a hedge of spent lilac trees, then through a grove of towering maple trees, down along a dirt path. The aluminum eyes from beer cans glinted in the coming light. We were heading toward the basketball courts, but there was a glow in the sky ahead, a golden aether in the morning fog where the courts used to be. Suddenly I heard voices. I thought he was taking me to see a flying saucer.

He stopped abruptly, just where the path turned through another grove of lilac hedges before the court.

"Wait," the Prince whispered, "I just want you to see. I don't want them to see me."

He pulled me up next to him and we crouched looking through the intertwined limbs of the lilacs.

It was like coming upon a camp of the little people, tens and tens of them on a square of the softest lime-green, the green surrounded by a border of what looked to be red clay. The golden light drifted up from the lime square, making a box of light in the sky above. Ten of the little people ran on one side of the square, chasing and tossing the ball and yelling so loudly I wondered how we hadn't heard them from Seneca, while another ten ran and shouted on the other half. There was music playing from two or three places and another whole crowd of them sitting around the perimeter of the square, talking and drinking, singing with the music, catching the ball when it got away from any of the twenty out on the green.

There were wee girls in the group along the fringes, some of them dancing and cursing, some kissing the sitting boys with full mouths. Sometimes a boy and a girl would wander off into the bushes behind the square; sometimes groups of boys would wander off alone and tiny fires, like lightning bugs, appeared in the dark.

"When?" I whispered to Jimmy.

"The city put the lights up after they resurfaced the courts," he whispered back. "There's an unspoken truce. The police don't hassle you if you stay near the courts."

He tapped my shoulder and started off back home, setting his feet down carefully so as to make no noise. I heard him hiss for me to come. I did not want to leave, it was like finding out that the Iroquois had come back during the night. The noise faded as we moved back through the lilac wood.

chapter three

political stirrings

Two days after the Prince emerged from his mausoleum, Black Peggy came home from college. She had to delay for a remedial course in English, although she wrote poems that had the grace of Keats. I asked her why they had made her stay.

"They don't read Keats in Westchester County," she said.

It was a good thing for Jim that she came home when she did or there would have been grumblings that he had only waited for her. As it was, my mother called it "the coincidence."

The Prince had come down the next day, just after I woke up in the afternoon. When I came down the third-floor stairs, he had called to me.

"Edmund, is that you?"

"Yes."

"Alright, I'll be out in an hour or so."

"Why not come out now so I can use the john?"

"I have to put my affairs in order for the hospital."

Jimmy was canny, I hadn't told him the parents' plan.

My mother was at the kitchen table, drinking coffee and planning things. She always plans in the afternoon, although she discriminates in it, worrying over the more distant reaches of the future. Dinner she plans at the last moment, it keeps her from cooking.

"Did you talk to Lazarus?" she asked.

"Or he to me."

"If he stays in any longer, I'm going to call the firemen."

I had threatened him with the firemen also on the first day. When I think on it, the threat is peculiar to the Irish, an indication perhaps of our trust in institutions. The police would not be called because they have guns, and also because their officers, at least in the past, were usually Italians. Firemen in our city are a home brigade, thoroughly green in number, although lately the Polish and the Blacks had been making inroads. Still, in our neighborhood, a Fire Chief, like my Uncle Joe, has the rank and demeanor of a three star general. When I was Jimmy's age and burned the kitchen down while making french fries alone in the house, the Chief's car paused only slightly after gliding to the curb. A fireman pointed to the house and then to me and the Chief nodded. The fireman was one of the Riordens from our neighborhood, who when the trucks first arrived, had stopped the others from axing away the upstairs walls, a standard practice. He said he knew us, and they put it out without chopping. The Chief's black eyes centered on me, and I was more ashamed than I had been running to the neighbors in my underwear. Then he nodded to the driver and they sped off.

Our admiration for firemen might also have to do with their methods of governance, the special anarchy congenial to Irish temperament. I remember also when the double-sized house burned down on Indian Church. It was the men from the hook companies I admired then as they sat, straddling the peak of the house like characters in Chagall, having mounted the roof as if they were off to the hunt. We boys cheered them,

56

my Irish firemen, heroes. They were calm there, high up, sitting and chipping away the roof tiles and the wood below, while we could see the roof popping into flames, burning just beyond them. Below them, other men moved in and out with the dragon hoses.

An anarchy of firemen seems a viable model, they work in associated groups like cells of terrorists. Even then I spent much of my time watching the Chief, his black suit cheap and clerical, white-haired, handsome-faced, the ritual bright metal hat; he talked in whispers, men came up to him and made, evidently, reports, then he spoke quietly into the black box. Everything centered on him, all this circus LaFrance, the fat canvas adders leaking at the couplings. With a wave from the Chief, the smokeeaters adjusted their masks and trudged, big boots in step, inside to look for life among the other things. A lace curtain burning like a silent scream. All that afternoon I thought of my father, but when I got home I couldn't think why and so didn't tell him.

"You won't need the firemen," I told my mother.

She looked up from her sheet of paper, covering what she wrote with her hand. I saw numbers there, and spirals—numbers not arithmetic—I think she was making a spell on the page, some numerology. I'm convinced my mother is a witch. Once we were talking about injuries, wounds and broken limbs—a friend of Brendan's had fallen from the cherry tree next door—and I said to her that it seemed curious that none of us eight had broken a limb. She smiled curiously.

"Not really," she said, "you're all protected."

Impulsively, I accused her then. "What do you do, cast a spell over us?"

She looked up very strangely.

"My prayers are answered," she said. "That, and you have strong German bones."

Even after she had said this, she studied my face as if gauging me. She knows I can sometimes read minds, it is something I learned from her when I was young and used to sit up late waiting for my father to come home at eleven-thirty after the middle shift. We would just sort of talk without talking. I mentioned it once, but she said I was imagining it. I didn't believe her then, and I doubt her more now. Despite her insistence on her German blood, my mother, like Peggy, is Black Irish mostly.

"He tell you he's coming out?" she asked me.

"No," I lied, "I have a feeling."

"Well, just go back up there and tell him if he's coming out he'll have to wait for your father to wake up before he gets his ride to the hospital."

"I can take him," I said.

She folded the sheet of numerals and put it among the papers in the file that sits at her feet under the kitchen table. She writes things regularly and puts them there, but shows them to no one.

"Not while your father's alive, you can't," she said, "He's been savoring this moment for days. What he'll tell the doctors . . . He'll give them the family history and then diagnose your brother for them."

I laughed and poured coffee, sitting at the table with her, talking and watching while she worked her crossword puzzles. The afternoon light in the kitchen was yellow on yellow. Whenever my mother has had the complete choice about a room's color—the ability to do it over without regard to the existing furnishings or my father—she has always chosen yellow. At first the kitchen had been only partially yellow, from the panelling on up the first time it was painted after the fire, and then wholly yellow when the old refrigerator was replaced with a lemon-colored one. And yet my mother never wears yellow herself. This too is the curse of the Black Irish complexion; perhaps complicated by some Germanic disposition, a fondness for more somber apparel. In a way it is too bad she does not wear the color. On a large woman, such as she is, it would be compelling, walking out like the sun itself.

Whenever I am home, I know an afternoon will come when I will sit in the kitchen and talk with my mother alone. Such times are something each of us children have in turn and never think of, except Deidre, who once went back to school in a scalding huff because Moira had interposed herself in a kitchen talk, obstinately or jealously refusing to leave, even after Deidre said she was trying to talk with my mother. What had angered Deidre most was that Moira condescended (her patience and parenting extend even to other adults), sitting next to her at the table and saying, "We know you are lonesome sometimes, DeeDee. Don't we, Mom?"

"It's impossible to be lonely when you're around, Moira," my mother said. Moira misunderstood the irony, but the remark comforted Deidre enough that she remembers to tell it with the story.

Even though I know the talk in the kitchen will come, it surprises and pleases me when it does. It just seems so unlikely that in the midst of the chaos events will slow enough that there is time for my mother to give me her attention. I know this is an infantile response, in an exact sense, but what is remarkable is how persistent it is. I had trouble lying about Jimmy, or rather keeping his confidence, because of the persistence. For when I talk with her there, I feel a deep magnetic compulsion to tell her everything. She even laughs about it. For as far back as I can remember, I would blurt something to her, something Colleen had told me in secret, something Brendan did and he was afraid of, and she would laugh and say I was a blabbermouth. Still, she would take in what I told her, often doing something in my presence later that let me know she remembered Brendan's fear, Colleen's worry. It was in that sense that I would confide in her, as a mediator, a negotiator, as someone who could barter confidence for confidence.

I suppose I should be afraid of that, but we Irish have never observed the psychological niceties about Oedipal situations. "A son is a son until he takes a wife, but a daughter is a daughter for all of her life." My mother quotes this proverb, but I'm certain she does not believe it, or, if she does, that she bends the belief to suit herself.

Perhaps she understands it in the sense that women are

teachers, the original deities, and that a son passes from his mother's teaching to his wife's. I do know, from chancing into the kitchen when she was talking to one of my sisters or my wife, that there is something unique in what she speaks about with other women. This is nothing new, I understood it always, preferring when I was young to stay in the kitchen at parties and listen to the conversations of my mother and aunts. I asked Mary once what she and my mother talked about, after they had spent hours together at the table.

"Oh nothing . . . " Mary said, "you know, kids and things. How she used to worry about you."

Mary keeps little from me. I think she was telling the truth, that as far as she could recall they *had* only talked commonplace. Yet I know, in the way I know with Mary, that she learned things there, important things. Maybe, it is only that the teaching differs, more a way than a thing. My father is the thing-teacher. For as long as I can remember he has drawn diagrams and made charts to explain the answers to what seemed simple questions. I take after him in this, priding myself when my blackboard illustrations are undecipherable by the end of the hour.

My mother looked up from her puzzle. "You boys are too sensitive," she said, "that is, if anyone cared what I think."

"Well, it seems we're not sensitive to that, to what you think."

"Touché," she said. "You know what I mean."

"Jimmy's got a lot of pressure. He's the last."

"You sound like Pat, with that crap. He's always brooding around when they come for dinner, cause everybody's gone. At Christmas, I told him to hire a family if he felt that bad."

She thumbed through one of her crossword dictionaries, then another, finally penning-in the word. She works her puzzles with a black pen.

"We didn't raise you to keep you tied," she said.

"You didn't raise us to abandon the family."

"You sound like your father."

60

I was surprised. I hadn't thought that my father was considering these things, that he worried over the shrinking. The way my mother said "your father" had signalled a turn, one I wasn't sure of. The tone was the one she used to worry over him, but what she said suggested a complaint. She has both worried and complained to me as long as I can remember. The Irish directness with the Oedipal dilemma is, in this way, a practical thing. The children, and especially the eldest son, become resources for a concerned mother, a sort of "Paddy, go to the pub and get yer Da" reflex. It is also a way for a child to learn to become an adult, prematurely to be sure (once, having to write a biography for employment, I wrote: "I cannot remember when I was not older"), but effectively.

My father behaves in a similar fashion, but with him it is, understandably, a conversation about a sweetheart we have in common. "I worry that your mother is tired," he'll say. Often they play an Oedipal drama upon the screen of my personality, especially during phone calls, which divide cleanly into his or hers. If I call and he answers, she comes wearily to the phone after we've talked, and I have to be careful to save special tidbits for her. If she answers, she disappears without a goodbye if I ask to speak to him. It is worse when one or the other calls me, especially if she has called and he gets on the upstairs extension.

I waited for my mother to show her hand. First she bluffed.

"How's Mary feel sitting there alone at the edge of nowhere with an infant son while you run home to soothe your neurotic brother?"

"That's hardly a question one can answer while retaining any dignity," I said.

"Damn Doyle dignity," she said.

So that was it, the complaint and the worry. She was upset with my father for making a production of Jimmy's swoon.

"How is he?" I asked.

"Pain as usual," she said, understanding exactly. "Still, he gets up lately at the goddamn crack of dawn, then sits around trying to figure how soon he can wake me. Then the pain drives him back to bed, and I'm downstairs here trying to figure out why I'm awake."

"He wasn't up at the crack of dawn," I said, flirting with telling her about Jim, then retreating from it.

"Nearly. Ten o'clock is dawn when you go to sleep at five."

I got up from the table to make some eggs and fried potatoes. She continued to work on her puzzle, but when I sat down she said that the eggs looked good. I served her what was left from the pan, having made enough for her in the first place, even though she had claimed she wasn't hungry.

"I wish he'd go to the damn retirement dinner," she said. "They broke his back and wore him down, the least he can do is get the damn watch."

My father had decided not to go to his retirement dinner the following day because of Jimmy.

"Anyway," she said, "it will be good for him to see some people. He goes crazy here with us. Your brothers get him mad."

"I did too," I said. "We all did."

"It was different," she said. "He had his strength."

I thought she was going to cry. Like any Irish boy, I would do most anything to keep my mother from crying, especially crying there at the table, wiping her eyes and swallowing the tears, making deep sounds, helpless as a bassoon.

"Jimmy will be out," I said. "He told me."

She wiped her eyes and then her glasses with a tissue, then blew her nose in it.

"If only he wouldn't keep sticking his nose in the boys' affairs," she said. "They'd grow up on their own."

"Peggy worries him," I said.

"Peggy's a girl!" she said sharply. "She's got her own troubles. She's a pain in the ass, but she's just a girl. You all had girl friends, you just didn't have your father to help you."

"I know," I said softly, "I know. It's just that Jimmy seems so tied up with her. It keeps him away, even when he's here."

"Maybe what your brother needs is exactly to get away more. He's too tied up in things here."

62

She hobbled to the counter and poured more coffee, and on her way back grabbed another pack of Chesterfields from the cupboard.

"Anyway," she said, sitting down again, "how would you know about that. You're not around here enough to know that."

It had come around full circle, from being blamed for coming home to being blamed for not coming home enough. She was right. I didn't know Peggy well, although I'd met her the last time I was there. But that was in the first days, when Jimmy and Peggy were first starting up and it was understandable that they spent so much time out together.

"I wish he'd get out anyway," she said. "I keep telling him to join a camera club, or play cards, or do something."

She meant my father.

"Get a girl friend?" I asked. I was teasing, being naughty, trying to emulate Pat's charm with her.

"No," she said, sternly, "not that. Besides he's not strong enough."

There was a basket of sweet-rolls going stale in the center of the table. My mother leaned and grabbed one, nibbling it gently like a bear in the zoo eating an apple.

"How *does* she feel?" she asked.

I know no more about how Mary feels when I am away than I know how she feels when I am there. It sounds unthinking or cruel to say this, but I know better, I know Mary very well. If there is one thing, however, that I learned from my part in my parents' drama, it is that you cannot know how someone feels, you can only know them.

I mean pure knowing. It is like the famous questions and answers of Sekito, the zen master. A disciple asked Sekito who had attained to an understanding of his master's teachings. Sekito answered, "The one who understands Buddhism." Said the disciple, "Then you've attained an understanding." Sekito said, "No, I do not understand Buddhism."

Mary is from the hills, from Kentucky, and in this way she

understands Japan, knowing the subtle contours. When we first met I attained some understanding of her, now I do not understand her. She is, in her own term, "simple," by which she means the hills she grew up in, a certain mode of existence. She is also: insecure, achieving, romantic, boastful, naive, complex, and always, always, courageous. She has a feisty kind of carriage, the look in the eyes of a habitué of hell by election, staying on even when the inhabitants would choose to flee to the mountains where it is cooler. She is vulnerable—something screams within her always—but she has the aspect of a jonquil, its toughness.

Mary understood when I went home. She asked the questions she always asks when we go there.

"Do you ever wonder how it would feel to be the youngest, like Jimmy? To always be doing something for somebody older?"

Then, when I do not answer, she says, "*I* know. I always feel strange there, when I ask for something and someone runs to get it. I'm used to being the youngest myself."

Later, she asks, "Do you ever think about how all you boys pick a girl and stick with her? Jimmy, Brendan, you and Pat; how young were you when you first had a girl friend?"

"Fourteen," I tell her again, although I may have been thirteen.

"Is it because of your mother, do you think?"

Before I got on the plane, while the baby was sleeping in my arms, she asked me, "Doesn't it bother you ever, the greyness there?"

"I've thought of that," I said. "Basically the pattern of presence there seems virtuous. Courageous. People stay and breed and grow there with a certain naiveté, despite the greyness."

"Like Moira? Or Colleen?"

I nodded. "Or my parents, for that matter. I suppose it seems a cowardly blessing. It is ugly there, and the people have that breeded into them, their eyes, their drab clothes, the sky even. There is a sense of, what can you call it, hemmed-in-edness?"

"Not the Doyles," she said. "The Doyles are beautiful."

She touched the boy's sleeping face.

Mary does not see that the greyness hangs like smog just beyond the rise behind our own paste house. She sees what is nearest. She does not like it here—she would rather be back in Iowa, or even Kentucky—and she has no friends, no real friends, only the women she dances with, arranges flowers with. But she is happy with what we are given here. She cannot understand my anger at the factories, my hatred for small appliances, especially since I do not lead a simple life, since I am too lazy to live without electricity or even the automobile, the shiny roach that brought us to the airport.

Mary does not know how I feel either, and so we have a good marriage; at least in the way I understand such things. For we work at knowing; when I call her I always think she will say it is raining there, raining in Japan; ask me: can you hear the rain? can you hear our son breathe?

My father took Jimmy to the hospital and they kept him overnight for observation; they suspected a flu. Even when he again claimed he was disappearing, they attributed it to exhaustion from the flu. There are always forms of influenza in the air in Buffalo, and I am led to think it is a spiritual illness on this account. To a certain extent, it is. Influenza does not always take root, it seeks a weakened victim, like ragweed thriving in thin soil.

When the doctors said that Jimmy would come home if nothing showed up overnight, my father decided to go to his retirement banquet. He called it that, a banquet, even though the invitation said a retirement dinner. Pat told him that he should wear a tux, and he got angry when Brendan laughed at him when he asked, "Really?"

"No, you should Dad," Pat said. "No matter what they wear. A midnight tux with a ruffled blue shirt, like Colleen's wedding."

"They made a puppet of him long enough," my mother said. "I won't have him laughed at."

She had turned testy, with Jimmy out and herself committed now to attend my father's banquet. She likes parties, but detests the time leading up to them.

"Perhaps he ought to, for exactly that reason," Deidre offered. "Not to be laughed at, but to show them he has survived them."

"For you," my mother said, "dressing up means wearing clean painter's pants. What do you know about dinner dress?"

Deidre folded. She dropped her fork on her plate and began to cry, pent up inside, like a cat. It is characteristic of Deidre to wither under attack. She thinks we are unfair and often brutal with each other, and she is right. She has too much sensitivity for us, being unable to understand when she is persecuted for other's sins. She is so sensitive in fact, that she never says goodbye when you call her, since she does not like goodbyes or any expression of overt affection.

She drew her hands to her face, clawing her forehead, the mewing weeping winding out of her as she ran from the table.

"See what you've done, Pat," my father said, also characteristically deflecting. "I'll be the judge of when I'm used and when I'm laughed at." He addressed this last remark to Pat also, but it was meant for my mother.

"Yes, sir," Pat said.

"Smartass," my mother said.

Miranda got up from her place at the table and went and put her arms around my father from behind.

"You would look handsome in anything, Mr. Doyle. Don't you worry," she said. "Wouldn't he, Mrs. Doyle?"

And my mother nodded yes, yes, and for a time it was better. Deidre and my mother sat talking all evening after dinner in the kitchen, and so that was better too, somehow, though I wished I could have heard how they patched it up.

There is a general consensus that my father was used; it is not just I and my mother who think so, even my father admits it. It is hard to say exactly how the plant used him, but we believe it. It is hard to say much about his life there. I know that he began when he was sixteen, working part-time and going to school, but I don't know much about those first years, except that he rode to work on a motorcycle. He rode it every day for two full years, until a friend of his hit a bump and flew up off the saddle of his bike and was decapitated by a power line, right before my father's eyes. "It toppled like a football." It was a story he told us when we wanted motorcycles. He had parked his bike on the shoulder and walked to work after the ambulance came. He never rode the bike again, but he could not afford to miss that shift of work.

I know that when they married my mother moved into the family house, making lunches for my father and his brothers, as well as their father, all of them working at the plant. There are stories about those lunches: how my mother fixed a sandwich that was all edges, huge slices of corned beef and cheese for my uncle Pat, and in the middle of the bread, in the bare center, she put a note, a sheet of paper that said, "This is a western sandwich, it has wide open spaces." Or how my father and Pat stuck toothpicks all around the crust of a cheese sandwich that my uncle Lou took to toast at work on the furnaces. They stuck in so many toothpicks that the sandwich was a lattice of wood, and Lou said it cracked when he bit into it. My father can still laugh himself breathless and red in the face thinking of that sandwich. I think the toying with food has something to do with their experience of the Depression. My mother likewise remembers coloring and rolling out one pound balls of margarine in a sheet, and cutting it into squares so they would think it was butter, but that was during the war.

Another story concerns my father, the plant, and Lou during the war. Lou is the ghost of my father's family—his real name was Donal but he was always called Lou, after Lou Gehrig, because Lou was quiet and dependable (or so my father says; my mother says Lou's mother gave him the name after birth, because he looked like her dead brother). Lou is my godfather and sometimes I think I am like him. When we were young, he once brought his daughter over to my mother's while my father was at work, and while we played with our cousin, Lou sat and said nothing. After four hours, he left, and my mother never knew what was going on. Lou died first of them and suddenly, instantly dead when his car hit a tree head-on at three in the morning. My aunt hadn't known he was gone. When they autopsied him, they found a brain tumor as big as a walnut. He was Black Irish.

I was away at school when he died and could not come home; my father called three times: once to say Lou was dead, a second time to tell about the funeral, and the third to tell me about a plaque he had found in Lou's workshop while helping my aunt with his things. It was hand lettered in Irish, in Gaelic, and used to hang in my father's darkroom, until it got mislaid: *Talamh gon chios agat/Agus bas in Eirinn.* "Land without rent to you/And death in Eirinn." It was a curious thing for Lou to have, he was a chemist, the most successful of his brothers. My father went to the Irish Center to have it translated, and ended up taking courses in Irish. He, Deidre, Brendan, and Jimmy took them, but only Deidre and my father recall any. They still all belong to the Irish Center and annually give money for medicine for Belfast.

"Bullets," my mother says.

Anyway, when Lou got married, there was a party for him at the Doyle house. Lou was home on furlough, just before he went off to the Bulge; my father was working at the plant, his back already bad enough that the army did not want him. Dad was working middle shift and by the time he got home Lou, Pat, and Sy were drunk. They handed my father a bottle of whiskey and he drank it, then slept all night sitting up in the chair with his work clothes and boots still on. Not terribly unusual except that Lou and Pat had taken the chair out to the curb after my mother went to bed, and my father did not wake until his father came home from working the night shift at the plant.

"Come on in and have a drink for Lou," my grandfather said. He had left the party for work with a bottle of his own, which he had worked pretty well down. The two of them came rolling in to the kitchen where my mother sat angry and feeding me my pablum. She says my grandfather kept sticking his thumb in his whiskey and giving it to me to suck.

68

I remember the strikes also, although not the one where my father was roughed up by company goons. What I remember is his taking photographs and selling vacuums and china; and I remember a picture from the newspaper in which everybody swore they could see him. There were a group of men in long coats standing next to a flaming barrel to warm themselves from the rain. My mother and my aunts said he was the man near the center of the barrel, but to my eyes, and Colleen's and Sally's, they all looked like Dad. In later years, of course, being a foreman, he was on the opposite side of the fence during strikes, locked in for their duration for reasons I have never understood. During the longest lock-in, the summer was the hottest in history and we picnicked nearly every day in the park with my aunt and cousins. The strike and heat both went on, and then the auto plants shut down because there was no steel. The park became an encampment, a continual come-all-ye, an Irish brigade. It was there I saw my first Irish piper, sitting in the center of a group of men and playing the union pipes, the chanter resting on his knee. He was a red-headed Kerryman and they said he had played at the Puck Fair and Pattern. My father was happy when the union settled well, for the supervisory wages and benefits were tied to the union raises.

What else? My father crushed his toes once when a crane gave way and set ten tons on the outer edge of his steel-capped shoes. The ingot only grazed him, but the tips of three toes were "pulp" according to the doctor. It must have been painful until it healed, but I remember only that it was the first time he had missed work with an injury (although in later years his back kept him out regularly); and that he carved away the toes from his three year old Florsheims to make room for the swollen foot. The last memory is strong enough to lead me to think that the sacrifice of the shoe was a severe hardship. I also recall an elaborate and inconclusive argument between my father and my uncle Pat. My uncle taking the side that steel-capped shoes were dangerous because they were apt to sever the toes in accidents such as this; my father propping his bare foot on the table in an attempt to prove him wrong.

It is hard to think of him angry at the plant. He did claim to have helped an angry mob toss a commie from the union hall, but that was not the plant, and it was the McCarthy fifties (although he recalled it with pride when we first began to turn on the war in Vietnam). He was, however, angry when they brought in a college metallurgist and made him his supervisor, after my father had spent three months training the man. It was during those days that I went upstairs to wake him for dinner and he woke saying, "Throw three bags of magnesium into number four furnace," which made my mother laugh when I told her.

He was less angry than proud when he found out that Pat used a phoney name with the other laborers in the strip mill the summer he worked there. Pat did not want them to know he was Doyle's son, because they all knew Dad and told stories about him. Another foreman told my father. When he confronted Pat at dinner, Pat told him he wasn't ashamed of him. My father asked him why then.

"Because they say you work along with the men. That you're a bastard but a fair one. I'm so damn lazy I don't want them to know I'm your son."

No, he wasn't angry at all until he came home for good, the green hard hat with "M. Doyle" stowed away in the basement. I think then he realized that that was it. Pension and disability checks the first of the month, the company magazine bimonthly, a retirement party to be scheduled in the near future when ten or more supervisory personnel had retired. Done, just like that, forty-odd years and there he was, home on the porch.

It is not surprising, of course, that there wasn't more anger along the way. It is hard to be mad at a corporation. Oh, there were petty annoyances, and even some deeper anger at injustices, but nothing in the spine. Then when it came, there was no one to be mad at. Not even the satisfaction that uncle Joe's brother-in-law had. A Scotsman, he used to work in Detroit, at Ford's as they called it. When the company laid him off for good, he spat curses about Ford's and it seemed that he meant a real person. My father had only Bethlehem, a town in

Pennsylvania, the name of an English nuthouse, the birthplace of the reigning godhead, a corporate shield. It would be better, I think, for the working man—what Jimmy calls, quaintly, the common man—if every corporation had an actual as well as corporate person. Someone to hate when they're done with you. Even the poor Iroquois had that.

They didn't give him a watch, they gave him a thermos bottle. Covered in simulated calf-grain leatherette, it had its own leatherette case with shoulder strap. Each of the men also got a silver pen with the company logo. We had made a banner to hang in the front hall when he got home: "Happy Retirement Dad."

"We should add a line saying, "May your bones heal!" Brendan said, but Sally shut him up.

We sat having champagne and ham sandwiches and he showed us his gifts.

"Now who in the hell would use something like that?" he said.

"It's for football games and fishing," Pat said.

"It's for suburban executives," my father said.

He pronounced the word with five syllables: ex-ec-u-a-tives, mouthing it with a slight tang of irony. The word is one of two that he pronounces with something near a brogue (it's natural that he doesn't have one, born in Pennsylvania), the other is *beautiful,* which he gives full ride: be-you-tee-full, speaking it for flowers or reproductions of great works of art.

He was turning the bottle around and around, his face red and shining, he had had a good time.

"Now wouldn't this frost you," he said, pointing to the bottom. "All steel and made in Japan. Now there's the story."

When we were younger he would never buy a foreign car, they were "made of tin"; but when he and my mother got interested in camping, they bought a Volkswagen bus. "I made the steel for these things," he said. "I know how strong they are."

He passed the thermos around for all to see.

"Seven sippings over Tokyo," Harry joked.

"Maybe Edmund should take it back with him," Miranda said, quickly trying to cover Harry's bad pun. Sometimes there is the feeling that the Doyle spouses compete for the family's attention, take care to keep the others from embarrassing the ruling party. The thermos returned full circle.

My father offered it to me, holding it out with his arm.

"You want it, Ed?"

"No, Dad, you earned the damn thing. Fill it with champagne and go camping."

"Champagne'd ruin the metal," he said, serious as ever.

"Matt," my mother said.

"But we will go camping. I was thinking of it anyway, now that . . . ," he paused. How to speak about Jimmy.

"Now that Jim's abandoned the Jakes," Jimmy said, beaming.

Pat laughed quite loudly. Pat and Jimmy are each other's audience.

"I missed the chance for a great one," the Prince explained to Pat. "All steel and made in Japan. Noh, there's the story!"

Pat laughed harder still, and Harry surprisingly joined him. He had been thinking of the same joke.

"I don't get it," Colleen said.

"Like Noah's ark," her husband explained.

The Prince and the Chief laughed louder.

"We'll see about camping, when we see how you feel," my mother said. "He wouldn't go dancing after dinner," she explained to Miranda.

My father never dances, never did, even before the pain. I've danced with my mother at all my siblings' weddings and my own; she moves with the grace of a cloud, like a huge cumulus.

"No, we'll go tomorrow," my father said.

"Said the ark captain's spouse to her mate," Jimmy blurted.

He was working on variations of Noah-Noh-Now, what is known in the family as sending up a squadron of jokes. We laugh at the idea of it, to keep pushing a bad joke.

"Matt," my mother said again, this time using his name in the soft way she does.

"The trailer," he said, but then he paused and beamed, " . . . The ark is in the driveway, ready to go."

Jimmy, Brendan, and Pat rewarded him with a laugh.

"Yes, and the Prince is reigning again," Harry said.

I watched my mother. In the middle of all the laughing, her face had gone suddenly pale, her eyes concerned and a little afraid. She was watching my father, and when I looked I, too, saw that he was in extreme pain. He had been laughing with the boys, his face turning redder and redder, his jaw wide open, but now he was frozen in that mask, breathless with the pain that had struck him. For a moment no one else realized it.

"If you wait a day, me and Peggy can go," Jimmy said.

"Matt," my mother said, concerned.

By then everything was silent. Everyone had frozen, aware now of my father. Pale blue patches, like clouds, surfaced in the red complexion of his face and neck; he sucked in a deep, long breath. In the midst of this driving pain, I thought calmly: heart attack. There was an element in this return of mine that presupposed that one of them would die; it was prideful to think this, an auxiliary anxiety really, as if, yes, I'm here now so you can.

"Matt, are you alright?"

He had let his head drop toward his chest and he breathed slowly, deeply, clutching his thigh muscles.

"Yes, damn it, yes," he whispered. "Brendan, get me a darvon."

The pain eased slowly, elastically. He took the darvon and then poured a glass of whiskey. My mother did not even warn him about alcohol and drugs, the pain was that bad. The party meanwhile dissipated around him. Although we all remained there, we talked quietly in pairs, watching him from the corners of our eyes.

"Too much up on my feet," he said, puffing the words out.

Pat looked up. "Jimmy's jokes can be killers," he said softly.

Brendan choked on a swallow of champagne, laughing with

relief. He choked and choked, until he too turned white, and Miranda was ready to give him what she called the "hug of life." But then his breath caught again, and he began crying, taking the tension for all of us.

"We'd better get going," Pat said. "You can try out that hug of yours when we get home to twin-sheets," he said to Miranda.

My mother feigned shock and said, "Oh Pat . . . "

It was better then. My father insisted they would go off and camp the following day. I decided to wait another few days there, ostensibly for the party which Sally suggested. "We'll have a buffet and stuff while they're away," she said. But I think I was also waiting to see what would come, to be there if something should die. I decided to leave sometime after my parents returned.

My father refused to go to bed right away. Instead he went up and worked for awhile on his darkroom, making alterations, putting up panels. Calmly again, I watched him, thinking he'll work himself to death tonight, he has that capability and is near enough. But after sawing and piecing in one section of panel under the sink, he either gave up or decided he had proved enough, and excused himself and went to bed.

That night before sleeping I had a pre-dream of him as a husk, not a person but an aging thing, plant or animal. It was a peaceful, threatening thought. Not surprisingly, I dreamed of him later, a dream very much like the one he told Deidre. His aquarium had spilled and I was picking up fish from the floor, from pebbles, and so on, launching them again, saving my father's fish. Some of them swam athwart, obviously going to die. Still there was the effort, finding fish where I had not looked before.

Most often my dreams are this transparent, this comforting.

chapter four

civil unrest

I will confess this much: I had no overt philosophy until we came to Japan. Before then life was formless, although that too is a form. My brother Pat and I have discussed this, how you have to grow away from the family to understand the formal aspects of its unselectedness.

We were talking about seeing. Pat said he was struck by how beautiful the world is, its array. He was talking about the decline of illusion, of Maya. "Illusion had its charms," he said. "The danger, the incredible seductiveness was that it was so sensual, sensual enough to release you from the contemplation of pain. The egolessness of it all!"

"And now?"

"Look at the ads in the Sunday *Times*. They are not so much sensual as motivational. What they offer are luxuriant spaces. Their appeal is to people crowded, inhumanely, into New York boxes. I mean the so-called middle classes. The irony is that those who can afford luxuriant spaces are those to whom it does not matter."

"What about us?" I asked.

Pat laughed. "We grew up in the Milky Way. Cosmic clutter. That way you grow to appreciate even a corner that has nothing in it."

He could have been describing the Japanese. They appreciate space here. Lately in our district the towns have begun to exhibit an American phenomenon, as buildings are razed to graded lots of gravel and broken brick in the center of towns. Nothing is to be built on them, they are just old, empty spaces. Soon automobiles will nudge against each other into loose rows on the cinders. But for now there is space, the surface of the moon in the center of a town. In one such space near here, an old man sweeps the sand and stone into patterns like a zen garden, combing the sand into soft, constant waves. Lately trucks from the engineering firm which is preparing the lot for a nearby bank have been parking on the lot, destroying the patterns. They are a sign of what will come, here as everywhere. And yet, every evening when the trucks leave, the old man returns and makes the world new again, at least within that space. I have thought sometimes to tell my father about him.

What happens, like with a Japanese garden, is that you become conscious of what holds things together. Conscious of relationships. This was how I found my philosophy.

I was sitting before a suburban teahouse inside the spring sun, eating an Uji Ice and watching a woman with her two children, a woman alone. I was thinking: she literally holds them together, gathers them up, in her vision. It is her concern which keeps them whole, keeps them from whirling away in a spatter of fatty molecules.

The children linked hands and turned about a ginkgo tree; the shaved ice in my lacquer bowl sighed and slid further into the green tea syrup. I thought: we cohere, as do the trees, or the stones of the teahouse walls, by an energy. I realized then that I could become the most impossible of philosophers, a Platonist, thinking that the idea of things holds them together as much as their event.

I thought of the stonemason I had watched, repairing our

courtyard, days before. Thought: real bricks increase in weight according to the energy applied to them by the brick-layer. He had held them lightly, as if they were weightless as balloons, chipped them to fit by cradling a single brick in his hand, his chisel in the other, and watching the empty space closely, letting his eye form the fired clay. The ginkgo tree existed as the children and I saw it to, the energy of our seeing holding it together.

I had learned something about my family.

On our honeymoon, Mary and I had hired a car to drive around Ireland and we were surprised to see that tinkers still travelled the country roads in horse drawn caravans. My parents camp like the tinkers, their small hump of a trailer laden with things—too many pots and pans, odd tools, lawn chairs, gadgets. What is different is that they do not hang their tinware from hooks on the exterior of the car, and that a low and leeringly dark blue automobile pulls their caravan. Also they do not travel from village to village, but from city to a point nowhere, where a park is provided for them to stop.

Only Jimmy, Brendan, and I were home when they left, and we watched them turn the corner with some of the anticipation that death must have, for we were looking forward to the party, the first full gathering of the family without my parents there. But we watched also because leavetaking is an elaborate and sad and satisfying ceremony among us, this one more poignant with me going back, and my father's pain fresh in our minds.

They had put off going for a day while my father regained strength. That night I sat late on the porch with him, in silence, while unbeknownst to me, and probably to himself, he planned his crime. He had given me a present, the leather bound book of Emerson's essays which had been his award for the best essay in Greek for his high school yearbook. He made me promise to have it rebound, and inscribed the flyleaf, "From a former scholar/Love, Dad."

"Hardly a former," I said. "You still read. You have your

darkroom and photographs. You know as much about Jimmy's astronomy as he does."

"I don't," he said. "That kid knows his stuff. That's the damn shame."

So, it was I who had brought up the subject of Jimmy. In a way then that makes me an accomplice. My father meant that it was a damn shame Jimmy did not go to school; he meant Peggy; and, by the bye, he meant that he had meant what he said, a former scholar. That it was up to me.

He had apparently been a brilliant student. The family story is that he was going to go to MIT, that his great uncle had offered to pay his way, but then his family made him refuse the gift. The great uncle was strange, he had a picture taken of his wife in her casket. My father's mother disapproved and she convinced her husband. There had to be more to it, but that is the story. The result was that my father went to a year of college at home, played soccer and studied the classics, working in the plant the whole while. After a time, they needed money. My father didn't go back to school. Lou became a chemist, Sy and Pat doctors. My father contributed what he could and became an amateur pedant, to the point that it eventually bored his younger brothers. I recall watching my uncle Sy talk to my father at uncle Pat's wake. They were talking about vitamins—Sy's a disciple of Vitamin C—and my father went on about his medicines, about the benefits of the B-complex, his cult. When Sy spoke it annoyed me how he condescended to my father, quoting from "the journals" about "comparative rates of diuresis"; but I saw also how Sy clung to him, and somehow thought him wiser. When someone would come into the kitchen Sy would literally dance to keep within reach of my father, his eyes going blank with lonesome helplessness at the interruption. It was especially bad when one of uncle Pat's neighbors came in—she had never met my father—and she caught her breath in a muffled scream at my father's resemblance to Pat. It is as I said: the Irish view a wake as a genuine rite of resurrection. The woman almost fainted. My father and Sy had both seemed hurt by the mortality of resemblance.

"Emerson was Japanese, you know," I said to my father, trying to turn the subject away from Jim.

"No, I didn't know that," he said. It was embarrassing, I had been trying to make a subtle point about Emerson's sensibility, using my knowledge of his fondness for orientalia. My father had either not listened, brooding about the Prince, or taken me at my word. I didn't explain, we watched the night.

"Your mother is sick to death with worry because of that girl."

"She worries about you too," I said. I wanted to say it was the same way, that he misunderstood her about Black Peggy, that she was only trying to do what could not be done for either of them—ward off the coming pain.

"No," he said sharply. "I mean it makes her sick. She has trouble breathing. I want to get her to camp so she can breathe."

I thought, she smokes too much, she's overweight, sometimes she seems to be breathing with difficulty but she is only thinking.

"There's good air out in the world," I said.

"Damn it, neither of them do a damn thing around here. He and Brendan," he said. "You always pitched in, you were always doing things, cleaning up."

It was a lie, I said so.

"I didn't."

"You always did."

It was decided. Nothing I could say would prove it.

"They're not going," he said. "I want your mother to be able to breathe without that little girl around."

"Jim said they couldn't go anyway. Peggy has to go somewhere with her mother this weekend. Mom asked him."

He launched a cigarette butt from his thumb with a snap of the forefinger. It lofted toward the street like a miniature sky-rocket.

"How did Pop meet Dolly?" I asked, trying to change the subject. Dolly was my father's stepmother, my grandfather had married her late, when I was still in grade school. I didn't want to ask my father about his natural mother; we all believed that they didn't get along, that she lorded over him, her boy, then turned on him when she turned to booze.

"She was one of his gang. A whole gang of them. Your grandfather probably gave her a line about having money. They needed companionship. I didn't like her very much."

Two surprises there. The first about Dolly, I hadn't really known that he didn't like her. Dolly was a powdery woman who spoke in an affected accent, quasi-British. She claimed to be a Mormon and wore flowery silk dresses. I have a childhood memory, a comic trauma, of a family party at our house, a first communion. Brendan was showing a new basketball net to his cousin, one of Sy's kids.

"I have a bat and a ball," he said. "I have a bat and a ball."

Dolly was bringing a plate of food to the living room, moving past my uncle Pat. "He's got a bat and two balls, Pat, doesn't he?" She giggled wickedly. "A bat and two balls."

Pat's nose was bright red, his eyes clouded with laughing tears; he had been entertaining the cousins in the living room.

"He sure does, Dolly," uncle Pat said.

Dolly lived with uncle Pat and his wife after Pop died.

The second surprise was the note of disdain for his father. My grandfather Doyle was a regal man, given to white suits of seersucker, with suspenders, and wing tip shoes in two colors of leather. When my mother first met Pop, his arm was broken. He told her he had fallen from a white horse during the St. Patrick's Day Parade. Only later did she find out that he had fallen from a barstool at Maloney's. When I was a child, he would take me there and buy me birch beer and pretzels while he sat and talked with his friend Joe Ketter. I still remember their starched white shirts and golden cuff-links, how Ketter told me about when the streets had wooden sidewalks. Pop also used to feed me sardines and pigs' knuckles, and every St. Patrick's Day he sang a doleful song that went:

Irishman, Irishman, hang down your head
Take a look at your country, and wish you were dead

Take a look at your country, and there you will see
How dirty and rotten the Irish can be . . .

He would hang on the baritone note of the final "be-e-e-e"
and it was always an event for laughter and applause, profane
celebration. So, too, my father sings Auld Lang Syne each
New Year's, it is an event for tears and awe. It was likewise
moving when my father sang "Red River Valley" or "You Are
My Sunshine" to my mother. Once Pat and I had, by chance, a
maudlin conversation in a suburban bar in which we com-
pared grim wishes: the songs we would sing at our father's
funeral. He chose the valley, I took the sunshine.

"Pop was a sweet talker," my father said. "He had a load of
bullshit."

I couldn't understand. I had never heard my father speak
so. I thought: maybe it is Pop's charm he remembers, the
obsessive sweetness. My mother always talks about how Pop
would come home from working middles while my father was
working nights. Pop would sit and talk to her and to my aunt
Kitty, keeping them up to the middle of the night. Then,
when they had given up on impressing him with their fatigue,
he'd leap up and say, "As Samuel Pepys says, and so to bed . . ."
and be gone. Night after night he did this; I wondered if my
father grew jealous of this time at home with the women.

But his vehemence became immediately clear.

"That's part of Jimmy's problem," he said. "He's a sweet
talker too. That girl brings it out of him, she encourages him.
He winds around her like a honeysuckle on a stinkwood."

I tried to joke. "She smells alright to me."

He turned to me. I could see the streetlights in his eyes.

"Oh, she's a sexy little thing," he said, "like all the Black
Irish. And never did a day of work in her life. I could murder
her for the pain she causes your mother."

It was oddly discomfiting to see his mad lamp eyes. I tried
once more to turn him away, this time choosing mild agree-
ment.

"Not to mention the pain she causes her own mother," I said.

"There you are," he said. "I'm counting the days until she goes back to school."

He reached into his breast pocket, where he keeps his pens and lifesavers, and pulled out a thin book, like an address book. It was insane, he actually marked the days.

"Sixty-three days," he said.

"That seems short," I said, resigned to the madness for then.

"They go back early anymore," he noted, matter-of-factly. "In late August."

He lofted another sky-rocket and prepared to go in.

"That's what's wrong with America," he said. "The bosses and the bankers have the working men all doped up in sex and what-not. Nobody knows about work anymore. You just dance to their pleasure. No wonder Jimmy lost his rocker."

I was aware that my father, too, had lost his rocker at that moment, that the forced adhesion of his front-porch socialism to the situation of Jimmy and Black Peggy had made him certifiably mad; but I was too impressed by the truth of his analysis to want to quibble the mild madness of its misapplication. My father the Fenian Marxist, I thought, Maude Gonne would've loved you! He went inside like the wrath of god.

Looking at my sister Sally, during the surprisingly quiet, even listless, family party we had with my parents away, I saw that she had become a woman, someone with a familiar adult face, as if she were one of my aunts seen by my father during the parties of our childhood.

Like most people, I do not enjoy thinking of mortality, my own or anyone's. I do not mean death, itself a fascinating and obliging subject for speculation, but rather mortality, the inevitability we share with freshly cut flowers. Aside from my occasional dabbling in the sutras, where mortality, and death, for that matter, are treated with the dry, poetic reserve of musical criticism, my only real indulgence in mortal matters is my admitted fondness for muzak. Even here it is difficult to convince the most remote acquaintance—let alone myself—that my sympathy is not a variety of extraordinarily retrained cynicism. Yet muzak—the song not as song, but rather as pure language, as mere occasion—seems to me incredibly sweet in its sadness, and worthy of respect. I am especially fond of that variety of muzak which is broadcast in one or two places on every FM band. Which is, in short, intended for those who actively seek its melancholy out of both a deep need for and a dread terror of silence. For, unlike the programs broadcast into elevators and public places, this commercial muzak (or "beautiful music" as it is packaged) seems pure in intention. It is more place than time, more mathematic than atomic. In any one hour of this programming, there come ten or more melodies which are instantly recognizable, instantly evocative of a particular time and place that is no more. I take this evocation to be the most profound sense of what one means by mortality. A friend once said that until his wife left him, he did not understand who the songs on the radio were written for; but on these beautiful music programs one's wife is *always* leaving or gone, whether in the arms of another or dead beneath a vase of freshly cut flowers. Proms are over, weddings have lost their glow, friends transfer and move away, children grow into strangers against their and your will—all this is meditated within the purity of these songs. It is a music of the past, including the past that will be.

I saw this same sense of mortality in my sister's face that evening. She reminded me of Aunt Kitty, Pat's wife, whom I had last seen at a not dissimilar party months before. I remembered that we sat in the kitchen of her house, a whole group, the society of my parents and aunts, all of them intertwined and yet each of them having become the characters they had always been in the stories. "Speaking of typewriters," Kitty said, and no one was, but we did thereafter. She seemed more beautiful than I remembered her, but also more hurt and confused. The party would be the last event in her and Uncle Pat's house, she was moving to an apartment. Her daughters were there that night, my cousins, like my sisters, having become women, in this case a social worker and an immunologist. I made jokes with one of them, and the jokes were as fair an approximation as I could make of the jokes my Uncle Pat used to make to his brothers' wives.

Watching Sally, I thought that much of the listlessness at our party seemed to result from an almost unconscious attempt to pattern our actions after those of our uncles and aunts at similar occasions in the past. It was all the same, even to the menu. Ham and beef—both sliced; rolls and butter; potato, macaroni, and green salads; baked beans; jello salad; and pickles and olives in my mother's platter which had always been reserved for pickles and olives. There was something sad and noble in the table, the macaroni salad no different from one I might have had twenty-five or five years before: seashell pasta, tuna fish chunks, celery crescents, all in a waxy mayonnaise, but tasting splendid, as perfectly balanced in its texture and flavor as an elaborate tempura. A much better case may be made for the achievements of working class cuisine in our country than can be made for the virtues of muzak, and yet both are deeply unappreciated. Even my mother cooked with grace and exactness for a family buffet.

Still, there was that mortal listlessness, that sense of impersonation. Sally's face brightened into her mad-girl Irish smile only when the talk turned to children or the ribald doings of the Stranger.

If any of us is likely to make the political act of having a large family, it is Sally. She and Harry have what seems to me an admirable marriage, for they have founded it out of mutual respect for each other's oddnesses. Sally was driving a truck when they met, not quite a real truck but rather one of the small aluminum-sided chuck-wagon trucks that cater to construction sites and sell coffee and snacks. Harry was one of the carpenters who worked on the same crew with Chief Don, the genuine Iroquois carpenter whom Sally was dating then. Chief Don said not a word, neither in the presence of our family, nor—according to Sally—in the relative intimacy of an automobile parked at a fast food restaurant, which places were the locale of their only dates. When my mother asked why Sally kept going out with him, Sally displayed the mad-girl expression and burst into laughter.

"He's so funny!" she said, "I laugh and laugh at him, and he just sits there chewing on his naked burgers, never batting an eye."

It seems that the Chief liked to get done up in his deerskin cowboy hat with beads and turquoise on the band and drive out for a dozen hamburgers. It was his amusing habit to strip the meat from the buns, sailing the circles of bread out the window, and eating each disk of meat held daintily between the index fingers and thumbs of both hands. Needless to say, Sally was ready for a more engaging companion when Harry began to linger at the truck.

Harry, however, was not ready. His first marriage was ending then, unfairly, and Harry could do or say little about it but instead wept without provocation. At first he began to weep by the truck, and then later to weep when he and Sally would go out.

"You go from a loony who doesn't talk, to one who does nothing but cry!" my mother complained.

We knew that something serious was developing when Sally defended him, saying he was only a little boy at heart and that he needed someone to be there. Sally had been the second mother to us all—older and younger alike—and we knew her feelings about little boys.

"He won't even sleep with his feet outside the blankets," Sally told my mother. "He's afraid that monsters will eat his toes."

My mother ignored the obvious implications and said only, "I think you're going to marry him."

"Naw, he's a jerk," Sally said, "besides my feet get too hot," and she laughed aloud.

Nonetheless, Sally began to invite him inside the house. In the beginning she had made him wait on the porch when he picked her up, made him flee from the door when he brought her home, even on New Year's Eve when she came home at eleven o'clock, explaining that it was a special occasion for our family and that we restricted it to relatives only, neither being true. These threshold precautions were taken because, as Sally explained before their first date, "He's ugly, and married, and one of my 'patients' besides. I don't allow my patients to enter my residence."

Sally's intentions finally became clear a number of months after Harry had begun coming inside the house. She could no longer contain herself and confessed the cruelest of her pranks to me, The Buddha, Pat, and my mother one night around the table.

It had started with her laughing uncontrollably as Harry followed my father from the table and out onto the porch. She laughed so hard her face turned blue.

"What have you done to him?" my mother asked.

Sally laughed again, gesturing frantically to The Buddha, and finally getting enough breath to whisper, "Go and see if you can hear what they're saying."

While Brendan spied, she confessed to us. Harry had asked to marry her a month before and she had accepted, providing that he meet her father's "requirement" of asking for her hand and detailing the dowry he was offering.

"You didn't!" my mother shrieked.

"Shhh . . .," Sally whispered and lapsed to laughter again.

She calmed long enough to blurt, "I told him that's why I stopped seeing Chief Don . . ." By this time we were all laughing madly. She croaked some more of the sordid tale, "I said that Dad had been angry about the dowry . . ."

The situation was, of course, intolerable, and Brendan, Pat and I set out to right things that very evening. We tricked Harry into leaving his pursuit of my father by ambling onto the porch in the middle of a conversation that seemed to be about the state of the economy, and which in retrospect we imagined was some of Harry's groundwork for the matter of the dowry. Once on the porch we said we were going out for a beef on weck at what we knew was Harry's favorite place, a prospect we were sure he could not pass up. That night over beers we explained to Harry that our father had authorized us to settle the matter of the dowry, and assured him that he would settle for one dairy cow, or the equivalent value in cash, which we explained to him had been the standard dowry in the old country. He seemed relieved, and they married a few months afterward. We gave them the dowry back as one of the wedding gifts.

On their wedding night, Sally left the reception two hours later than she and Harry had planned because she could not bear to break away from the piano where she sang with us boys. Later that night, according to Harry, she cried because she missed us. But once that night passed, she and Harry made the marriage of their oddnesses, and began to concentrate on the huge family that she said she wanted and which they had begun in what must have been among the most remarkable of all first conjugal embraces, with the both of them crying madly, since Harry could not help but weep along with her. Thereafter, all has, at least on the surface, seemed well with them. For, if Sally becomes exasperated with him on account of one of his oddnesses (say when he forgets that he is feeding Sean or the newest baby, and reads oblivious while the infants scream), it is balanced by Harry's ability to accept her sometimes craziness (for instance, the time they drove all night on the way to their summer cottage and Sally became convinced that Martians had replaced Harry with a robot that looked like him, and she refused to talk to him for two full days afterward).

And, most likely as a result of his stalking of my father in regard to the dowry, but just as certainly as a result of their workingman's compatability, Harry has become the closest of my father's acquaintances. A shame to us, but a friend to him, in the time when we had begun to lose sight of my father.

And my sister smiles when the talk turns to children, but laughs aloud when it turns again to bawdy, and either way redeems us from what passes for mortality.

The Stranger represented a peculiar sort of bawdy. Perverts of one kind or another have, in our neighborhood, like any lower class enclave, held a mythological if not holy position. Not just the madmen but the mad-and-dirty are reported at regular intervals. They become the subject of teachings by parents and teachers and the objects of hunts or, at least, public ridicule by the legal authorities and able-bodied adolescent vigilantes. In my time, I remember several. Herb is still around. He is known for allowing anyone who wills to punch him as hard as they may in the stomach. His stomach is a taut, pink, ovate thing that he carries before him like a man walking a balloon. His posture is very straight and his legs sinewy and tight and so the stomach rides high. This predilection would only make him mad, but what makes him mad-and-dirty is not only his appearance (he is round-headed and bald but for black strands of hair that he combs across his skull, and he wears wire-rimmed scholar's glasses), but also his total accoutrement, which gives him a sleezy and sexual air. For in summers he wears only a pair of swimming briefs of the old fashioned velveteen variety and within which his genitals are slung like giblets in a bag; while in winter he wears walking shorts whenever possible in the snows, and pleated khaki pants otherwise, always without jacket or coat, wearing only very white teeshirts and rubber shower thongs on his feet. When he is punched, he grunts vacantly and says thank you and walks on. Of course, neighborhood wise guys throughout the years (even now I wonder who first punched Herb, how it came to be known; since when I was young, the older kids already knew) have attempted to hurt him. Punches to the groin he always deflects with a neat and balletic lift of the knee to cover the area, but once I personally saw a mean little fellow, a classmate of mine by name of Jimmy Proctor, fool him and come high, the punch making an odd, wheezing sound as it crushed the diaphragm. Herb bent clear over on top of his own stomach and vomited, remaining bent for at least ten minutes while the crowd around him either laughed or felt sick themselves with the horror of it. After a time, however, he straightened up, said thank you, and walked away.

Other perverts have been of the more common variety: pure exhibitionists, candy purveyors and dirty talkers, laundry thieves, peepers, and one or two collectors or dispensers of effluvia (an old woman who threw feces, a middle aged man who stopped his car and asked boys and girls to spit in a coffee can of sputum for money). A few have been simple criminals, rapists of one variety or another. Few, however, have matched the elaborateness of Herb.

The Stranger threatened to. Universally called that by kids, parents and priests, he had been working the neighborhood, but mainly the park, for almost a year, with his encounters increasing in recent months. No one had really seen him closely enough to identify him, since he almost always came upon someone in the dark, whether on a path in the park or along one of the side streets in the space between the pools of streetlight. Also he usually wore a hat, either a forty's style fedora or a duck-bill cap of the kind my father fancied. It wasn't really certain whether The Stranger was an exhibitionist.

"Linda Martin's sister said he pulled it out," Jimmy said.

"No, Jim," Black Peggy said, "she said she thought he was scratching it while they talked."

Sally began to laugh here.

"How old is she?" Sally said. "There's a helluva difference between pulling it out and scratching it."

"Sally!" Colleen exclaimed, turning bright red but giggling nonetheless. This was the reaction Sally had hoped for.

"Well, there is," she said. "Isn't there, Harry?"

"Well, you have to start from scratch," Harry said.

Colleen turned redder, Sally laughed uproariously.

Black Peggy seemed to be the acknowledged expert on The Stranger, although The Prince and Brendan knew some things as did Bella. But Peggy knew most of all, which was strange since she had been away at school for nearly all of The Stranger's reign. Yet there was something about her that made her authority in this and other matters seem fitting; she seemed like she might be the queen of the little people. She seemed like Mary Queen of Scots slipped back from exile.

Generally, I do not look closely at people. For months I was certain my own son looked exactly like me, until recently I was surprised by his reflection in a shop window and I discovered that he is the likeness of Mary. Most times I ascribe my inattention to a disinterest in the transitory aspects of being, but really I think I am not generous enough to attend to others. That night, however, I studied Peggy carefully, for what now seem certainly obvious reasons, but which then I thought was on account of her mesmerizing presence. It may have been on both accounts.

Black Peggy is short, perhaps Mary's size, five feet. I was surprised by this, because I remembered her as slim and tall, maybe because I think of Jimmy as tall (he is not), or maybe because I remember most women as taller than they are. She seemed Mexican to me that night, partially on account of her sandals and gauzy blouse and shorts, but also because I increasingly notice that dark-haired young women and girls look Mexican. Blond girls conversely look Scandinavian. I am sure of this. It is as if, in recent years, the white, occidental world has reduced the broth of its genetic pool into two distinct types of women, the fair, cool northern women, and the dark, feverish southern. Both types seem remote and wonderfully mysterious. When I discussed this with Mary, she assured me that what I see is only my romantic vision of younger, more sexually precocious women. She says I am becoming middle-aged and that my illusion of the bright and dark ladies is endearing.

Nonetheless, Peggy's most prominent feature is her own light and darkness. Her eyes are too closely placed together below bushy black brows; the centers of them are like dark chocolates. The closeness of her eyes, and the broad ivory palisade of her forehead, combine to give her three main expressions: amused, puzzled, and shrewdly intelligent. Two additional visages are not properly expressions, but rather the lack of expression, or reposes. The first of these comes when she allows the chocolate eyes to unmoor, the whole of her pale, fair complexion becoming untense, with the exception of the faint chalky rill at the center of her upper lip, which quivers slightly. The rill seems one evidence that she may have suffered a slight defect of the upper lip at birth; the other evidence being a nearly imperceptible speech defect, hardly a

90

defect at all, but rather a hint of a whine or baby-talking, which is nonetheless endearing. This first repose is what might be called her naive one, and is nearest to her puzzled expression.

The second repose is no more than a variation of the first. It is her seductive or sensual face, which she exhibited whenever she and The Prince would stare into each other's eyes, and a final time just before she fell to sleep on the floor, her body curled into the oceanic curve of a shellfish. In this repose, her furry eyebrows seem to float up from the eyes, but her facial features remain untense, this time, however, also including the rill of her upper lip.

Her limbs are firm but somewhat bony in the Irish fashion, and her large breasts also seem firm, although they rest at such a slanting mound under her braless blouse that it is easy to mistake her as being less chesty. The flesh of her arms and legs is paler even than her face, and her forearms and extreme upper thighs exhibit unattractive black hairs, which paradoxically endow her with an aggressively sexual quality. Dusky lines of vein or blood vessel show themselves through the whiteness of her legs, and suggest that her legs may not age well. A prominent pulse throbs in the hollow behind each knee and at her ankles.

There is the suggestion of a fatty pad of flesh, an oval, at her abdomen. Her hair is long and crimped, black waves pulled up generally into a bun, parted in the middle in a bone white line. She wears no makeup and her lips seem rose-brown against her pale flesh. She has one jet black facial mole that I cannot place in my memory and which may in fact float about her face. She looks younger than Jim, with the exception of the depth of her eyes and the firm intelligence of her brow, rather than the five years older that she is. Finally, there is clearly an overall heat about her, the suggestion of a small, wild animal, or else I would not dwell as I do on her. A sexy, little thing, as my father said.

"But if he doesn't *do* anything, what does he do?" Sally asked.

"Talks!" The Prince and Black Peggy answered in unison.

From the way they responded it was clear they had been through similar conversations about The Stranger. It was as if he were their own creation, they sounded proud. Peggy had her amused expression.

"About sexy stuff?" Colleen asked.

"Listen to her," Sally mimicked, "Sexy stuff . . . Hey, honey, wanna talk some sexy stuff . . ." she growled.

Colleen's face was the color of the sliced, boiled ham.

Jimmy sat up straight on the floor, resting his arms across his knees. He assumed his bright-boy expression. Somewhere in his personality there is an angelic earnestness, which the rest of us have consistently stifled in our intercourse with him. With my mother, he shows it, and also with Peggy. Although in the latter case, it is something which we discover only by accident, coming upon them coiled in the living room and talking in murmurs. Jimmy and Peggy spend much of their time at the house coiled together on floors or sofa (and, one assumes, elsewhere), talking quietly and looking for all the world as if they are midway in foreplay. It is an adolescent pose, and does not gain them ground in the family favor sweepstakes.

"Not actually sexy," Jimmy said, "or not at first."

"With Billy Tucker he did," Peggy countered.

"That's Billy Tucker," Jim said.

The interchange was an envelope of private consciousness. The Prince continued.

"Usually he asks for directions somewhere. That's what got him named."

"Who named him?" Pat asked.

"Everyone," Peggy said, shifting to the shrewd expression.

Jimmy nodded. "Just all of a sudden," he said. "The court kids were the first to use it. It was like everyone knew."

"Court kids?" Colleen asked.

"The kids who hang out in the park," I said, urging Jimmy on.

"James wants to be one," Peggy snickered.

The Prince looked hurt by this disclosure. He rebuked

Black Peggy in a wonderfully patient and patronizing voice, a tone I recognized as the traditional Doyle tone for women, now going out of vogue for political and practical reasons.

"Hon, please," Jimmy said to Peggy, "let me finish this story, and then, if anyone's interested, maybe there will be time for me to clarify what I mean about the court kids."

"I'm sorry," she said, and went into the first repose.

There was a moment of clarified silence, during which Jimmy worked his Doyle eyes around her face. Then he went on.

"When you answer him, The Stranger strikes up a conversation. They say he's very good at it. It's very subtle. He talks about the night and asks more questions."

"My sister . . .," Peggy said, then covered her mouth, the chocolate eyes growing larger.

"You can tell, hon," Jim allowed.

"My sister even knew it was him, and she says she couldn't help it. She kept talking to him. He's very charming."

"But what's he *say*?" The Chief asked. There was a sympathetic grumble from everyone else.

"We're not trying to be difficult," Jimmy said.

There was another instant of clarifying silence, all of us chastened.

"Everyone knows it's not so," he said, "but it seems like he says something that fits everybody he talks to. I mean, he gets information from his questions, I guess, and then he uses it. Like, he'll ask what your father does, and say you tell him he runs a gas station. Well, The Stranger will say that your father is probably distant because so much of his life is spent waiting on people passing through."

"Kathy Boyle's father works nights at the electric company and he told her that her father and mother probably don't have a very satisfactory sexual life," Peggy said.

"But it's not just parents," The Prince interjected quickly. "He'll talk about you. He'll say something like that it doesn't make sense to fear death because it is only another dawn."

"Poetic things," Peggy nodded.

"Or private anyway . . .," Jimmy said.

"He's God," The Chief said. Miranda giggled.

"Damn close to it," Brendan said. "He told Billy Leary that he ought to wash his hair more. He said the rash on Billy's chest came from that. And Billy swears he never mentioned the rash."

"Billy Leary's a jerk-off," Black Peggy said.

"Bullshit," Brendan boomed.

"Wait," Sally interrupted, "I still don't understand what makes him a perve . . . Doesn't he ever do anything?"

"He asked my sister if she masturbates," Peggy said.

"No," Jimmy said, "that's not it at all. I mean, he does sometimes ask really private things. Mostly, though, he's strange because he's so . . ."

Jimmy paused for the word, he was trying to be exact.

"Intimate," Brendan said. He had ceased brooding almost immediately, the subject of The Stranger was that compelling.

"Yes," Jimmy said, "Intimate. He just gets into your life, and that bothers people. I mean, you know that's what he intends to do. It doesn't seem right. The court kids are hunting him for that, they hide out and try to capture him. They say they'll kill him."

"The court kids talk big," Peggy said softly. "They aren't so bad, they're just always hunting."

"The court kids think he's a commie," Brendan laughed. "Honest, they are really into that trip. They have a witch-hunt mentality."

"Come on, Brendan . . ." Jimmy's tone was placating but hurt. He was impatient with this, he and The Buddha must have been through it.

The pure charm of Jimmy's plea put The Buddha in an awkward position. The Prince had called him in front of us all.

"What do you call it?" Brendan asked, his voice growing loud. "You have a hard-on for those wimps."

"Please . . ." Jimmy said, remaining charming.

"Aw, bullshit!" Brendan said loudly. "Come on, Bella, I'll

take you home before he gets started on the community of wimps."

Brendan stormed out of the room with Bella and then Sally following after. We could hear them talking softly at the curb outside. The event signalled an intermission. Colleen and Fred also gathered up and left. Throughout the commotion The Prince remained sitting, having crossed his legs into a meditative squat, his eyes and Black Peggy's carrying on a tender and continuous exchange.

"Well," Pat said after awhile. Miranda had fallen asleep across his lap on the sofa. Harry, who had been paging through an old news magazine, looked up from the page. Jimmy responded quietly.

"Brendan might be right," he said. "I mean about the witch-hunt. Almost always The Stranger says something . . . It could be about somebody's parents, or if he asks you what you want to do when you grow up . . ."

"He's always talking about meaninglessness," Black Peggy said, "maybe in not so many words, but he always raises these questions. The kids don't like it. It gets them angry when they think how he doesn't respect anything. Like Jim said, he's too intimate."

"Brendan," Jimmy said.

"Whatever."

Pat sort of smiled and leaned back against the sofa, resting his hands behind his head. "What is this guy?" he asked. "A night-time Marxist?"

"It's just so empty, what he says," Jimmy said. "It can't be that empty."

"Did you run into him, kid?" Pat asked.

Jimmy did not pause, but I still do not know whether he lied.

"No," he said, "I just know what they mean. The court kids. They might be wimps, like Brendan says, but it can't be that bad."

"The Stranger is a bad man," Black Peggy said.

"It can't be," Jimmy repeated, "life can't be that bad."

I don't think that any of us were aware of Harry at that moment. One of his best qualities—perhaps it is an oddness actually—is what might quaintly be termed a quality of witness. Sometimes when he is among us, there is a sense that we interest him for reasons other than our highly contrived and complex familial personalities. You can almost sense him listening and watching, and sometimes feel that he is about to say something direct and even vaguely judgmental. You sense that he really sees us behind it all, that he likes us, that he really is (as he really is) someone beyond what we will let him be. I think this quality must be part of what bonds him to my father, I think they share this. Perhaps it is something that good men who work hard are able to do. Able to share.

For once Harry did not make one of his jokes.

"It can be," he said, putting down the magazine.

He stood and stretched, yawned.

"Not only can it be, it is."

He left the room and went out on the porch, calling softly to Sally. The Chief and The Prince exchanged glances. I looked at no one. The evening drifted away into morning in a sad wash of something like mortality. Harry and Sally left without saying goodbye.

chapter five

rebellions

When we were kids there was a game of checkers we used to play in which any captive piece is immediately transformed into one of your own color. Often this metamorphosis would get so out of hand that the strategy consisted in a test of each opponent's ability to recall which of the pieces before him was in whose service at the moment, together with an ability to argue, persuade or intimidate the opponent possessing either a faulty memory or a too accurate one for the changes. The method of attack—surprisingly like the Japanese game of *Go*, although much less complex—was one of slow intrusion, encircling, and subtle patterns leading to drastic and overwhelming shifts of force. Of course, the ability to menace and confuse an opponent as to the ownership of critical pieces was characteristic of the better players.

It was perhaps the only game I was continually good at, for life in our family had left me with both a keen awareness of shifting allegiances and an aptitude for debate. I never threatened an opponent since I was too weakly, nor did I resort to the common endgame of toppling the board in angry disgust, the strategy of neighborhood bullies. Instead I remembered. Remembered with an ancient's memory for relationships, and argued thereafter with quiet assurance. As best as I can recall, I never purposely lied about the extent of my holdings.

Even so I recall with desperation the times I lost those games, and the sickly feeling of impotence and disgust which accompanied the memory of what had been mine and now was turned against me. I imagine this was how my father must have felt in the days preceding his solemn crime.

Living on the outskirts, you become sensitive to shifting allegiances; or at least you should expect to, if you want to survive. The Irish did—we Doyles, for instance, were Welsh, captured and eventually made kings. The Japanese, too, made not just kings, but gods of their captives. Captives or conquerors: it is the same thing. My father should have known that too, but I'm certain he doesn't still. It makes him doubly damned.

Old Snake knew. Whether or not that is the name of the banished Iroquois murderer, my father's spiritual and real property ancestor, I don't know; but it suits them both. Old Snake knew who served whom. By the time the Iroquois came to the Buffalo Creek Reservation, Mary Jemison was an old and powerful woman, powerful in both worlds but more powerful in the new, Indian one.

Anyone who knows anything about the Iroquois (Deidre, for instance) knows that they traditionally did one of two things with their captives: tortured them gleefully, or incorporated them into the tribe. Incorporation was so widespread (so Deidre says) that in later years, after many wars, "the people took most of their texture from a weave of outsiders."

"The whole fabric," Deidre said, "had many colors, and Mary Jemison, being a woman, had a special place."

It is ironic and sad that this conversation took place in my father's presence. It was the morning of my last day there following Jimmy's self-entombment, and my father sat with us. That is to say, he had ample warning.

Deidre is an early riser, and I was up, in this early hour for our house, because I had to pack for the return home. My father had not been able to sleep through his pain. They had come back early from the camping weekend because of it.

Watching him at the table that morning, half awake but trying as always to talk about everything—this time with Deidre about the Iroquois, although his true subject as always was to catalogue his learning for his children—he looked like a fading gunslinger. An old snake.

Bleached yellow streaks of dull pigment stood out from his otherwise silver sweptback hair, his blue cloth shoes were frayed and pushed out from the sides of the gum soles; and both his dark sweater-vest and the chain-pattern yellow and white shirt under it (a shirt button gone at the belly) showed pale blue balls of lint, as if he had held the blanket around him after dressing and before coming down. His face was white from pain, prickly with a grey bristle of several days growth, and his eyes were the sad and cloudy blue of old bottles. Yet, even as he shuffled from the table to the coffee pot and back in his dark blue trousers (down now below the belly at the waist and on the shoe tops at the cuffs), he still retained a definite grace, a slow surety. He was an older gentleman, not reduced but relaxed to this state, cigarette after cigarette going yellow and cold in his fingers, his glasses frames glinting silver when they caught the morning light.

"Then it was a melting pot?" I asked Deidre.

"No," she said, but my father intervened.

"No," he said, "The melting pot is just the bosses' image. A sacred, industrial cow erected by pagans out of the slag from our furnaces of violence."

He spoke it like a snake, but like an Old Testament prophet also. His voice had been gummy with fatigue and slipping dentures, but the venom in it was majestic. I braced myself for

Deidre's anger; she is famous among us for her short fuse, and special intolerance of my father's more ornate pronouncements. (A fact I am sure he knows, and uses).

But to her credit, Deidre recognized the power in this instance. It is not that she dislikes him, rather that, like all the women in our family, she protects him, even from himself. This time, however, she seemed appreciative, restricting any intolerance to a mild correction.

"Not pagan, Dad," she said, "Protestant."

"Protty," he nodded.

She turned back to me.

"He's right," she said. "With the Iroquois we *are* talking about replacement rather than the euphemistic socialization."

"Hmmff . . ." my father snorted, "it's words like that which, . . ."

Deidre cut him off this time. She spoke loudly as if pointedly ignoring a child. My father repaid her previous kindness by suffering her interruption with a mild expression of interest.

"People were adopted to take the place of other people killed in the course of their capture," Deidre said.

"But . . ." I said. We had been talking about Mary Jemison and I hadn't thought her capture involved violence. Deidre cut me off as she had my father.

"Or to replace losses through natural death, or other causes," she said. "Shawnees traded her to Senecas, they adopted her to replace a brother lost in battle."

I realized that my father and I were nodding in time with each other, both chastened by instruction.

"And when you realize," Deidre was saying, "that Iroquois women held the real power, that they could seat and unseat *sachems,* the senatorial chiefs . . . that they trained shamans, and owned the longhouses, the fields, and the hoes to work them; and when you add to that what seems most important to modern eyes, that they controlled lines of inheritance and succession; they were the archetypal political bosses. The brother-in-law didn't stand a chance . . ."

I thought of them smoking cheroots, these wrinkled, chubby or angular women, sitting around a longhouse and discussing politics over baskets of grain, winnowing out the bad fruit and the weak men as they talked; laughing together, training daughters.

"It's like that damn Peggy . . ."

Old Snake's voice rose into my daydream like the sound of a steaming kettle. It seemed very far away and oddly out of place, but it was followed immediately by the shrieking whistle of the pot set off: it was Deidre, screaming in exasperation, leaping up, but unable to speak anything except a sustained and livid, "Oooooooh . . . !"

Allegiances had shifted. Old Snake should have seen it then in the meteor fire of his daughter's eyes. She had tipped the whole board over like the bullies, and my father should have known to get down on his knees and hunt the pieces which were his.

But he sat dumbfounded, a slight smile forming beneath the stubble of his beard, his lips wetting slightly in anticipation of a scrap. One more round.

It almost came.

"I swear if I hear those three words together one more time . . ." Deidre hissed.

But the steam built again inside her. She was stiff with anger, only her eyes hotly animate.

"OOOooooooh!" she said, "OOOOOoooo . . . OOhh!! OH!!

And then she was gone, clumping upstairs on legs wooden with anger, slamming her bedroom door, shrieking one more muffled, "OOOHhh . . . ," which we could tell woke my mother. We could hear her coughing awake.

Old Snake chuckled, a helpless dry, cackling laugh.

"That damn Peggy's got them all upset," he said. "They know I'm telling the truth."

We sat for a moment locked into a gaze of generations, snake eyes to antelope eyes. I wanted to run. Wanted even then to warn him.

"Just look," he said. "She's woke your mother again."

And he got up to prepare to take a cup of coffee to her, doing his ceremonies and heading off in serene silence.

He had meant that it was Black Peggy, Peggy who woke my mother then.

Talk about a double whammy! Mary Jemison was Irish to boot.

Deidre whispered this last news to me as I left the house. To this day I think I should have turned around right then, taken my father's arm, and marched him upstairs and out of the circle of them, to have a talk. To let him know how severely the deck was stacked against him. Even the ruling *anima,* the spirit of this outskirts, fronted him. No son of Erin resists Mother Ireland, I wanted to tell him.

It was impossible. Beside the fact that our variety of Irish do not do things this way, that sons do not advise fathers with any success; there were too many factors working against that moment. The cards were dealt, four face upward.

First, there was the circle of them, as many of the siblings and their mates as could be mustered for a farewell, as is our custom. Brendan and Bella, Pat and Miranda, Moira, my mother, my father, Deidre, Jimmy and Black Peggy. They stood in the front hall as if it were a wharf and I was sailing off. They were attentive to the whole process of farewell, watching each of my moves, taking each of my kisses, hanging on each of my remarks, as if awaiting a cause for weeping.

It is the way we leave anything in our family. We love farewells, attending to each moment of them as if gathering anecdotes for an elegy, a family history. Any abrupt move then—and especially one involving my father—and they would have followed me up, the whole troop of them in single file behind us, to hear the possible last blessing of patriarch and eldest son.

Second, there was the new news I had about The Prince and his plans.

Third, there was the fact that Old Snake himself was armed with new information. A letter had come from a distant aunt with an addition to the genealogy. There were gentry in the family, British gentry. Old Snake in his parallel life was the offspring of a Squire of Pennsylvania: Squire Cabot of the Cabots, farmers and mysterious gentlemen. He glowed that afternoon with the righteous fire and pride of a disowned son, as if, in his increasing rage at Peggy and the failure of traditional values, he had grasped in his very hands one of the walnuts which dangled between Squire Cabot's lordly legs.

Finally, fourth, he overheard her.

"Mary Jemison was Irish," Deidre whispered.

"Irish?" Old Snake questioned.

"Born on the boat between Belfast and Philadelphia," Deidre said indignantly, loudly.

"Belfast's not Irish," he scoffed.

And she stomped upstairs again, leaving me to leave in the silence of someone else's exile.

"It isn't . . . ," he said, sheepishly, to the hushed circle.

They looked upon him with embarrassment and shame. With silence.

"It isn't," he whispered now.

He was on slippery ground. Our standard practice was to consider the North Counties ours, especially in the matter of emigration.

"We know, Mr. Doyle," Black Peggy said.

He should have known it then: the exile done, his banishment begun. But the farewell took precedence again, and he was lost in the wake as my ship pushed from the dock.

"It's ours as much as theirs," he mumbled to me, when I embraced him, "This Cabot stuff confirms it."

It would be easy to say so many things. Since Deidre's throwing in her weight on Peggy's side proved decisive, it would be easy to say that my father was done in by nothing more than the old Doyle trait—and sin—of ignoring the womenfolk at the same time as one was acting in full assurance that one's actions served to protect and harbor those same women. This had been my peccadillo when with Mary among the Doyle and other urchins of Drumcondra that time; and it is also, most probably, why the chief gaps in my father's Doyle genealogy occur surrounding the women that Doyles married.

But Deidre—with her impatience—only accelerated what was already underway. Black Peggy was becoming a Doyle wife (although of the peculiarly modern unmarried sort), and Deidre was only doing what other Doyle women have done through the centuries: giving her welcome.

Deidre and Peggy got on awfully well considering the fact that Deidre did not especially like her.

The reasons for her apparent dislike were many, beginning with the undeniable truth that, of all our family, Black Peggy most resembled Moira in both appearance and demeanor. The Black Irish are apt to appear lazy, and Peggy shared that with Moira, so much so that I came into the kitchen during one of those days home to discover the both of them chatting calmly while a pot of soup boiled over onto the stove in a lace of golden fat.

"It's boiling over," I said, not intelligently.

"Peggy thought it would stop soon," Moira said, and they continued their talk, while I turned the burner down.

Whether Peggy's notion was that the volume of the soup would soon be reduced beyond the point where it would continue to boil over, or whether she predicated her belief on an extreme hope that the laws of physics would reverse themselves, I do not know. But I do know that they both had been aware of the fact. For I had no sooner turned the burner knob than Peggy swerved long enough from her conversation with Moira to say, "See, we knew it would stop somehow."

This sort of thinking annoyed Deidre, who herself is lazy but careful to avoid the appearances (although she rises early,

104

for instance, and retires late, she is careful to spend the post meridian hours of any day engaged in what she calls "reading," something accomplished unconscious and in bed). And I know for a fact that the instance of the soup annoyed her, because she scowled when I told her what had happened to the stove when she questioned me about it as she prepared to make tea.

"It's Peggy's soup," I said. "She and Moira left it there to boil."

"They are both such children sometimes," Deidre said, and she removed her tea kettle to another burner, carefully covering the lace-smeared burner with a large skillet, and thereby avoiding the appearance of sloth.

Another reason was that Black Irish are also apt to be vague in their mystic qualities, keeping their occultnesses inward, and giving the appearance of simple naiveté. Deidre, on the other hand, is a genuine but formal witch, a practitioner of Tarot and a weaver of eyes-of-god, which she imbues I think with formal spells.

"A tree flew away," Black Peggy said once, when someone asked her how she and Jimmy had enjoyed their walk in the park. That was her kind of mysticism.

"We were walking through the lagoon and a young tree by the creek started to flap its wings in the wind. The next thing we knew it wasn't there."

"Walking through the lagoon?" Harry questioned, perhaps understandably. The rest of us knew that the lagoon was the name for the lawn behind the casino where the actual lagoon had been filled, sometime in the early '40's.

"Trees don't fly," Deidre said acidly.

Moira was not there to comment, but doubtless she would have fought on Peggy's side. Black Irish are also apt to be stubborn, even when arguing on the side of the wrong. In fact, especially then.

"This one did, didn't it, Jim?" Peggy said.

"No," The Prince answered.

"Well, I guess it didn't," Peggy told Deidre.

This last instance, Peggy's immediate shift at Jimmy's advisement, was more than anything why Deidre did not especially like Peggy. More than the television (which Peggy watches every waking and non-dining hour); more than the fact that Peggy eats Japanese soup (ramen, which Deidre rightly detests); or the fact that she is addicted to Mountain Dew (which Deidre in a rare vulgarism calls, "sugar piss"); more—even—than Peggy's similarity to Moira; Deidre disliked the fact that Peggy played puppet.

It led to an irony. Up to the time that Deidre made her opposition to my father overt, it was conceivable that he might have imagined she was his ally. She wanted Black Peggy to give up on Jim; my father wanted the opposite; it looked the same to him.

An incident from the day before I left is illustrative. Jimmy was lounging on the living room carpet, his head upon Black Peggy's thighs. He was watching the finals of a contact kung-fu tourney on the television. My father skulked in and out of the room awaiting the segment on hurling in Cork which the sports panorama promised after the kung-fu. Deidre sat reading, her usual act of silent witness and vigil in the face of creeping televisionism.

"Get me an apple, hon," The Prince said to Peggy.

Peggy freed his head from her lap, placing a pillow under his neck as she rose. A sinewy black man fell to the canvas on the screen, chopped down by what seemed a glancing kiss from the foot of a modest sized oriental.

Deidre snorted in angry reaction to Peggy's submission.

"They're alright," Jimmy said, misunderstanding Deidre's noise, "it's mostly acrobatics."

"I hope it is mostly acrobatics," Deidre said to Peggy, "I'd hate to think you do those things because you feel you have to."

Peggy shrugged and left.

"Really," Deidre fumed to Jimmy, but he was intently watching the black man wring his head in his hands in the corner of the ring, trying most likely to revive his cerebral functioning. "Really," she repeated, "I expect it has always been that way from the first. Adam called for an apple, and the curse fell to Eve."

Jimmy seemed not to hear, which incensed Deidre even more.

However, even had Jimmy heard, I doubt he would have understood Deidre's comment with nearly the searing sarcasm she meant by it. Deidre has never fared well in argument in our house, for her taste in insult runs to this kind of arcane, and her temper is so awesome that she restricts it to a dry delivery and fast and frequent exits.

Enter Old Snake.

"You have no right to be together," Deidre snapped to The Prince.

"What's this about?" my father asked.

"They try to knock each other down. Fatal blows score a point," Jim said.

"They do indeed!" Deidre nearly shouted.

"When's the hurling?" my father asked.

Re-enter Peggy, with apple.

"Awfully soon," Deidre answered him. "I'm going to hurl one of these two out of this house before the afternoon is up."

"There you go," my father said to Jimmy. He was obviously buoyed by his daughter's apparent support.

I made the error of getting into the imbroglio.

"You don't understand," I said.

"Do any of you?" Deidre snapped, and left the room.

"Would you peel it, Hon? I can't stand these Delicious," Jimmy handed the apple to Peggy, who shrugged and left the room again.

The three of us watched the tube for an instant, secure in our separate truths. One of the contestants in this round wore a Cheyenne war bonnet but billed himself as an Iroquois from Canada. He faced another modest oriental. Deidre and Black Peggy were talking softly in the kitchen; the tone was sisterly and ominous. I had a momentary sense that we were witnessing, eyes and ears, the fall of the world as we Doyles had known it.

It would also be easy to say that we were indeed witnessing the fall of something larger—if not the world then our concept of it—and that my father's crime was one of those events which are not as precipitate as symbolic. This would seem especially so in light of the fact that by the time my father whispered it to me in farewell, both he and Jimmy had by their separate ways arrived at the knowledge that "it is ours as well as theirs."

What keeps me cautious, however, is that the each of them, not unnaturally, meant something different both about the "It" that was ours, and the "ours" that had rights to it. In fact, the only thing they did (and, I think, still do) agree on is the identity of the "theirs" who are popularly accounted seigniorial rights to the elusive It.

Since the politics get as complicated as the possessive pronouns here, it would be well to back up and give an account of Jimmy's news.

But first I should summarize my father's stance, as best as I can reconstruct it from that time. In short, he believed that Black Peggy, in her aspect as a formless and distracted Sybarite woman, represented the successful jettisoning of traditionally subversive anti-property working class values on the part of a protty, financial-industrial-radical cabal, whose chief interest lay in the assurance of continuous paralysis and stupor among that same working class. Further, he believed that Peggy's influence had caused, and continued to cause, an erosion in both Jimmy's moral fiber and his capacity for appropriate disenfranchised outrage, as exhibited chiefly in Jimmy's swoon, and in the evident disintegration of my mother's health both previous to and subsequent to the swoon itself. Finally, by a rather mystical but typically Celtic process, he linked Peggy's influence upon The Prince to the process of debilitation which factory life had evidenced upon him. Anticlimactically, he also believed—by virtue of the news of the Cabot heritage—that not only had the cabal usurped the rights and privileges of the working class, but also that they had done so illegitimately; that is, by indenturing even their own kin and thus claiming rights to the patriarchal inheritance.

He thought the solution to this servitude lay in an eventual rejection of the world of things on the part of the working class; or, more specifically, that Jimmy ought to give up on black Peggy and lead a proper (and therefore subtly revolutionary) life.

"They talk about wage slaves," my father expounded surprisingly during a dinner lull one evening. "That's where we had them!" He chuckled, as we sat goggle-eyed and expectant.

"We bought butter for the table and raised children," he summarized to the astonished gathering. "Nobody gave a damn about who owned what, until the bosses took over the unions. The whole capitalist castle of wax was in danger of melting away for lack of attention."

It seemed a wistful memory.

"Pass the peas," Brendan said, thinking that our father was done.

"Their castle sat in the glare of the sun," my father said, holding the bowl of peas within millimeters of Brendan's outstretched hand and addressing him, "melting away in the sunshine of public disregard," he said, "and the unions put up an umbrella and saved it . . . along with television and sex!"

Brendan pushed his gut upon the table and snatched the bowl from my father's prophetic fingers.

"That's the pure truth," my father said, as if spitting in the peas.

Someone—it must have been Pat—applauded.

"What was that about?" Deidre asked.

"Gibbon," my mother said, "the fall of Rome."

"Sounds like The Stranger," Peggy said.

Admittedly, another family would have worried about its Pap just then, and arranged to put him away. Perhaps our family might have, had it not been for the family mind. The family mind had supplied a context. The conversation just before the lull my father set out upon had concerned free agents in the athletic rather than the Aristotilian sense. The leap from free agency to wage slavery was not so difficult; and anyway my father had been taking a beating from The Prince in the discussion of baseball salaries and it was unsurprising that he would set upon a course of tactical confusion and bravado to hide his defeat. Old Snake had his wiles.

The Prince had his also.

"The Yankees traded Babe Ruth at the end," Jimmy said.

"My point exactly," Old Snake countered.

It was an Iroquois standoff. But the family mind had been ratified, and my father was saved a trip to Gowanda, the lake town where once the state hospital had been, and which remained the customary term for the nuthouse.

If nothing else, this standoff illustrated the iron will and orneriness on either side of this Titan and son struggle; so much so that this conversation leaped immediately to mind when, eventually, Jimmy gave me his news.

We had returned to the courts in the middle of the night, two days before I was to leave. It was Jim's idea to go back there, and it pleased me. I had wanted to see that green haze again but was afraid to ask. I worried that, if we went back, we might be caught and that somehow he would lose standing. I had imagined that it was a secret, that no elder was supposed to see. It was a measure of my falsely romantic notions. We walked right in.

After we had been there awhile, I felt comfortable enough to mention my apprehensions to the Cunningham kid, a friend of Jimmy's. I thought he would laugh at me, but he responded with solemn seriousness, vaguely shocked.

"I thought you guys wouldn't let me in," I said.

"But it's a public park," he said.

"See," The Prince said. I take it that he meant that Cunningham and the court kids were the finest representatives of the common man.

110

The common man. He had used that term repeatedly as he explained the basis for his decision. He talked to me from the moment we left the house, building his case, explaining what he wanted me to see that night at the courts.

"They are going after The Stranger sometime tonight," Jimmy explained as we entered the dark, druidic paths of the park. "I wanted you to hear them, maybe even follow along. I was afraid Brendan gave you the wrong idea the night of the party."

I was still too intent on my notions of the enchanted secrecy of the place to pick up on the suggestion that I might indeed follow along with them. My Welshness was rising, a genetic imagination: I daydreamed maidens with puffed sleeves and peaked, veiled hats; tiny steeds with silken armour; pugfaced fighting men and radiant knights and squires. It was a conscious indulgence.

"Watch for thorns," Jimmy said.

We moved through first the lilac hedge and then the maple grove and I tried to spy the smear of light which I was certain would disclose itself to a more experienced visitor to the courts. But there was nothing until the last lilac barrier; even the sound of the several radios was swallowed up.

"They're good people, they are. You'll see," The Prince said as he pushed through the barrier and walked onto the courts.

I followed involuntarily, propelled by the momentum which he had established. Jimmy's gait changed as he hit the red clay perimeter of the courts. He shifted from a considered, pacing stride to an almost liquid swagger, a black (what they used to call negro) walk, a graceful and sneakered glide.

"You made it after all," a voice said. It was Peggy, there before us.

I blinked to focus on her. The light within the courts was a dazzling green, brighter even than the box of light had seemed at its perimeter.

"Was there any trouble?" I asked, still stupidly worried about Jimmy.

"I didn't think you'd come," Peggy said, and walked off.

My vision began to clear itself. Jimmy was introducing me to people: Billy Leary, Cunningham, a Moran, and Dante and Butch Mendola, the red-headed Irish twins born of an Italian mother. The Mendolas had been to the house before.

"You remember Butch," Jimmy said. "His name is really Horace."

The group of them laughed, but it was not meant to hurt the Mendola twin.

"Sorry," I said, "I didn't recognize you. This light takes getting used to. It's . . . "

"Oz," Billy Leary said. "The emerald city."

He was playing hoop at the moment, so he ran back on the court.

Jimmy must have recognized my bewilderment.

"They don't read that much," he said. "The allusion is the same one everybody makes. We kids were brought up with the movie."

"Step back and you lose, monkey man," Peggy said, explaining. She had returned with a joint, which she handed to Jim.

"You mind?" he asked me.

I was sure he would catch hell from the group that remained with us, that they would mock his concern.

"Why should I?"

"Well, you're my brother. You might not want to sanction it, you know . . . It's a responsibility . . . " Jimmy explained. The others nodded gravely.

Cunningham picked up the slack silence.

"So you're the Professor?"

"Balding," I said.

He laughed appreciatively.

"From Michigan?" he inquired. "That's right, isn't it?"

It was an extraordinary feeling, this conversation. Cunningham addressed me like a distant uncle, trying to recall the facts, trying to assure me that Jimmy had talked about me.

"No," I said, "Japan."

"Oh yeah, that's right . . . Jimmy told us about that deal."

112

It was then that I had confessed my initial apprehensions to Cunningham, since he had made it clear that he was someone I could trust with my illusions and fears. He was a gelatin faced kid with knots of acne at his nostrils and temples, a curly brown afro atop his head like a war bonnet. I felt a solemn wisdom in him, a solicitousness that reminded me of my uncles, my father's father.

When Jimmy spoke his "See," Cunningham was sucking on the joint, but he raised his eyebrows in salute to the common man.

I found myself grinning, even taking a ritual toke from the joint as if it were a peace pipe. I hadn't smoked weed for years, but I liked this ancient little bastard.

"Well, let's get it on," Black Peggy said.

It was only then that I realized that I had not been introduced to any of the band of wee girls. They crowded around Cunningham, Leary, and Jim when Peggy spoke. She was their queen, although Jimmy was not the king of the court boys. Not surprisingly, it was Cunningham who led the briefing.

"Is all this for my benefit?" I whispered to The Prince as Cunningham began.

"Let's say they waited for you as an honor," Jimmy replied. "It was planned no matter what."

Cunningham was momentarily silent, watching us. I was afraid he would rebuke us.

"Are you ready, Professor?"

"I'm sorry," I said.

"Oh no! No," he said, "you can talk to your brother."

"Thank you."

My apology pained him, his face took on an odd pallor, .blushing in the greenish-yellow light. He stuttered slightly as he began.

"The girls will be the bait," he said, "but we've got to have three guys with every one so's if there is any fighting to be done, we got enough. Okay?"

No one answered, and the boys moved not at all; only the wee girls nodded, solemnly, dreamily. They were grim as terrorists, which in a way they were. The plan, as Cunningham described it, was to spread out into the neighborhood and the park, having each little vigilante squad concentrate on an area exactly one block away from a previous Stranger sighting. The squads detailed to the park were to stay at least a hundred yards away from where he ever was.

I raised my eyebrows; the detailed planning surprised me.

"A football field away," Jimmy whispered.

"Yeah, that's right," Cunningham said, overhearing.

"Any questions?" he asked.

"What if we have to kill him?" Billy Leary asked. Others nodded. Jimmy scowled.

"Then call the police," Cunningham said, "and send someone for the rest of us quick. We'll be witnesses and explain."

Although the trust in the designated powers was heartening, I felt a more than mild discomfort at the turn things had taken. I feared that, if I let the episode pass in silence, I would be an accessory to a crime; and, more importantly, that I would fail in what Jimmy had identified as my responsibility. I was going to speak, but I realized that either I had forgotten or had not been told Cunningham's given name, and it did not seem right to call him Mister.

He saved me the trouble. "Any suggestions, Professor?" he asked.

"Well . . . yes. That is, I mean I have a question."

I am sure that all eyes were on me, but I was aware only of Peggy. Her face disclosed an only slightly disguised amusement; it was a version of her seductive repose. Suddenly I had the chilling feeling that this whole scene had been organized to humiliate and mock me; I had a paranoid fear that The Prince had set me up, and that as soon as I took them seriously, the whole band would burst out laughing, thus satisfying some mysterious desire on Jimmy's part to punish me. The formless guilt of the moment made my skin run

114

clammy. I peered into Peggy's amused eyes in the way a would-be skater looks over new ice, and when I spoke I too stuttered slightly. I was even afraid that they would think I was mocking Cunningham with the stutter, and that they would be even more merciless in their subsequent derision.

"W-what do you plan to do with him? The S-stranger, I mean . . . "

It was hardly an ethical or moral imperative, but I had raised a question. I held my breath and waited for them to laugh at me.

No laughter came. Only the blare of the radios filled the silence.

Then Black Peggy laughed. I sucked in another breath and awaited the onslaught.

She laughed alone. It stopped.

"Whata you laughing at?" Cunningham demanded.

"I just thought it was about time somebody asked that," she said.

Cunningham was flustered and unmoored, I felt sorry for him. It was as if he had taken on the whole blast of ridicule that I had expected. He stammered a moment and then addressed me.

"Should we do something?" he asked, gravely concerned, "I mean, you got an idea for what we should do?"

"Torture him?" Billy Leary suggested.

One of the Mendola twins hit him on the side of his head, a single whack with an open palm.

"Yeah, we'll make him talk to you," the twin suggested to Leary.

Thankfully, everyone laughed. It gave Cunningham time to revamp. His face lit with a deep, confident grin.

"I gotcha, Professor. I wasn't hearing you right when you said. Thanks."

Although I didn't know what he thanked me for, I nodded crisply. Once again he instructed the troops.

"Like the Professor here says, remember our plan. Don't

get too heavy with all this killing shit. Just take it like we talked about."

He looked for my approval. I was dumbfounded, not knowing how to proceed. Jimmy spoke.

"My brother probably wanted to know about the plan."

"Jeez . . . "

Cunningham was plainly relieved. "You mean, if we get him?"

I nodded again.

"We'll bring him back to the courts," he explained; and, when that did not seem to satisfy me, he added, "We'll search him and ask him his name to see if he's telling the truth."

Again Cunningham sought my assent.

"He wants to know what you think that'll do," Jimmy said. He was right.

Cunningham spoke without an instant's pause, getting his answer out just before a deep and profound doubt settled visibly upon him.

"He'll stop then," he said. "Once somebody knows who he is, then he won't be The Stranger no more."

The doubt hit, but the show was over. The squad of wee terrorists moved off to what must have been predetermined stake-outs. Cunningham and his party—the Mendolas and girls—the last to leave. He walked rather confusedly, coming back briefly almost as soon as they left, to say goodbye to me and shake my hand. His face looked like that of a defeated general.

The Prince and Black Peggy remained, sitting crosslegged at my feet. I had stood to shake Cunningham's surprisingly plump little hand.

Cunningham's party moved away through the lilacs and the trees with the sound of a group of elfish woodsmen off to a hidden glade. Long after the voices and the sound of cracking twigs had receded, the fey music of someone's radio hung in the air. When they were quite gone, I turned to Jimmy and Black Peggy.

Her head was on his lap and her hand moved in swirling little gestures between the buttons of his shirt. I caught myself

116

feeling annoyed and mildly indignant at their seeming lack of propriety. I had reacted like Old Snake. These were two sexual little animals, even here, under the Oz light, sitting on the spongy surface of the court.

Without a word, Black Peggy kissed him and ran off into the darkness around the courts. Unlike the woodsmen, she made no sound as she passed through the trees.

"What did you think?" he asked.

"She didn't have to . . . " I gestured toward where Peggy had disappeared.

"She did. It's our talk," he said.

I sat next to him, aware that I now sat where Peggy had, a curiously incestuous feeling. I leaned back and looked up through the light, or tried to.

"The stars aren't there," I said.

"Light-fogged," he said. "There are never any stars in this city because of the light. Or at least not as many."

"They were really organized, Jim. I was impressed by the way that kid got the posse together. The whole plan."

"It's just television. They learned from Kojak," he said.

"Still . . . !" I wasn't sure why I was protesting. It had been impressive, their earnestness.

"What?" he asked. "Were they mature about it?"

His tone accused me of condescending, the way he lightly accented the word, mature.

"Yes," I said, "I think they were, even if you are setting me up."

"I'm not!"

The plaintiveness brought me up again, sitting, looking at him.

"They think," he said, "if they find out his name, he'll go away. It's all television. Or nightmares . . . just find out what the secret is . . . "

I could not follow his thinking and I told him so. It was evidently something he had been working out for himself.

"What do you think the police would do, if they . . . " he paused, "if *we* kids called them? It's a lost vision of America. The cops'd arrest *us* for mugging him."

"So?"

"You want to know what you're supposed to say?"

I nodded. The Prince yawned, it was a weary painful yawn, anxiety pressing with iron palms on his chest, pushing the air out. He began to laugh at himself, a private joke. I asked him what he was laughing at.

"Considering The Stranger," he said, "and the way he seems to always want to point out the sad things; I started thinking that *he'd* probably confess if the cops arrested the kids for mugging him. It's an upsidedown world . . . "

I laughed then. He sounded like my brother again, the strangulation of the yawn had released him. He gave me his news suddenly.

"I'm not going to college," he said.

I confess to more silence at this disclosure than I would have wanted, more certainly than I ever let pass when an occasional student of mine makes the same statement. I told Jimmy what I tell my students (even knowing that among the Japanese any failure to progress—even from kindergarten to the correct school—is a matter for suicide).

"You don't have to know what you're doing now," I said. "This isn't the age to know that. That is, if there is one."

Jimmy, however, surprised me. Unlike my student-san's, he reacted without relief. "I do know what I'm doing," he protested.

He had popped the bubble of one of my more insulting wisdoms. He was right; I did assume that my students also didn't know what they were doing. My unconscious presumption was that they would find themselves and be back. It was elitist of me.

"I'm going to try to stay with the court kids," he said.

"You can't," I snapped. "They'll get old."

I was surprised again. This time because he had angered me in finding me out.

"You know why they come here at this time of night?" he asked. His voice was measured, he was consoling me. Teaching me.

118

"Because the cops leave them alone. Because you can get away from stuff . . . from home."

"That's only part of it," he said. "Mostly, it's because they can't get on the courts earlier. In the afternoon and evening. The older guys—the ones who were the court kids before these ones—won't let them play."

I began to nod, and he grinned, it was dawning on me.

"You figure you'll grow into the afternoon?" I asked.

"Sort of," he said. "I want to be a common man, you know? That sounds funny, but I mean I'm ripped up by the whole thing. Part of me is them . . . Cunningham, Billy Leary, all those guys. They'll grow up and get jobs and marry somebody from the neighborhood, and go to work or get laid off, have kids, watch teevee, and then . . . "

He paused—still too young to speak about death comfortably enough to include it on a list like this.

Suddenly he was grinning again.

"You know what?" he said. "I like what you said about growing into the afternoon. Maybe that's it . . . maybe you grow earlier when you get older."

He laughed aloud. I asked him what he meant.

"Ever go around this neighborhood in the morning? What did you see?"

"I had a paper route," I said, "but I was never awake enough."

"You go to someone's house, or you walk by a porch in the summer, and fathers are always awake. Just sitting there in their tee-shirts. So many of them work nights. It's when they're alone. In the morning. Not even when they go to the bars for beer . . . "

"Then they should die in their sleep," I said. It was unconsciously cruel. "I mean if you follow the logic backwards enough."

But the cruelty hadn't touched him, he had left the subject for another, his main one.

"That's what I wanted you to see," he said. "The court kids are just like everybody. All this talk about catching The Stranger, telling his name, and everything. Later on, they'll want to bomb Vietnam, or restore capital punishment. They're like everybody with their dreams and fears and all . . . "

"Bullshit!" I said. The naiveté had caught me unaware, touched some furiousness I hadn't remembered possessing. The way he said "Viet-nam" was quaint. He was condescending to me. Still, I tried to back off somewhat, to mellow my reaction. "I mean, you got a tad too philosophical for me there," I explained.

"I know," he said quietly. "They do the same thing you did when I get carried away."

"Who?"

"Them," he said. "The court kids. It's the part that's confusing me. I always start thinking things like that—or maybe I get carried away talking about astronomy; or even worse, poems—and suddenly I realize how dumb it is to talk to them about it. They laugh at me. I wish I could be stupid."

"So does everyone," I said. "You can't."

"I know."

"No," I contradicted him gently, I wanted to be sure he understood, "I mean you personally can't."

"I know that too," he said. "I think about it everytime I'm around you or Pat. Even Brendan. We're different. We're smarter and we can't help it. The Mendola twins said they didn't understand any of the jokes we made when they were over the last time. I told them we really know the jokes aren't funny."

He went silent a moment, it was clear he was thinking something painful.

"Sometimes," he said, "I can't stand the crap I hear here. Cars, and dope, and beer, and how they're gonna quit school and go to work at the plant. It's so dumb . . . it makes me sad."

"Well . . . " I said. I didn't know what to say. He *was* ripped up, torn exactly in two. All the rough edges fluttered before him.

"So I'm not going to college," he said.

120

"What, to punish yourself?"

"No, to see what I can do to change it. It's their world too, right?"

He really wanted an answer.

"Right," I said softly.

"So maybe I can do something with myself."

"Those are school words," I said. I decided to get tough with him, to see how well he had thought this out. "To 'do something with yourself' is what they say in civic classes, in social sciences."

"*You* know!" he said. The toughness had penetrated some, he sounded hurt.

"Do I?"

"I hate all the fucking teachers who always tell me what a fine mind I have. They say it like I'm not one of the worms, you know. Not like all these people."

"It's called a meritocracy," I said. "You said so yourself. They're dumb."

Now he was wounded. "Do you think so?" he asked softly, "Really?"

Only then did I realize that the iron palms were upon my chest. The anxiety raced through my veins, I could hardly breathe. I knew then that we were also talking about me, about my father. I remembered that the world was real and not a place of jade light.

"Of course not," I said. "I think you're a saint. Really, you sound like a whole tradition: St. Francis to Marx and Lenin, but it won't work. It never does. There's classes, Jimmy. Real social distinctions between people, and we slid through the gap somehow. Our DNA strip unlocked the space between the bars."

"It's worth a try, isn't it?" he asked.

When I drove up to our house, only the horses remained awake. They stood each facing eastward against the breeze, looking like three ancestor-monuments in the wash of my lights. Mary and the baby were together sound asleep. Even the wind chimes were still; she had wrapped paper around them.

I lay down on the mat and cradled them both to me; I tried to bring sleep to my mind by retracing the moments, the miles, of the trip: walking through each instant from the last farewell in the hallway to seeing the stone horses at the end of the drive. Mary touched my eyes with her fingertips. She was awake.

"How was your father?" she asked, whispering to avoid waking the boy.

It was a strange thing to ask at first, but Mary knows me.

"He said the family was communism," I said, "that the three of us here can overturn everything. He says we have the strength."

"Isn't it?" she whispered. "Don't we?"

a martyr
and a saint

It was late winter or early spring: March. The long distance lines were unusually crackly, other voices and a low howling wind could be heard in the echoing background, whether in the house, the microwave relay stations, or the coaxial cables, I did not know. My sister Colleen was on the phone in the midst of these scratching spiritual howls.

"Murder . . ." she was saying.

"He what?" I fairly shouted.

"He shot a bank branch."

"Then why charge him with murder? Has it come to that already?" I asked.

The background noises whirled me up, like Macbeth's witches, and for a time I could not hear Colleen. Our baby clawed at my legs, saying "Up, up, up . . ."

" . . . terrible, and we don't know what to do about our vacation with the trial coming up . . ."

Colleen's voice surfaced on this sea of troubles like a woman

sunbathing on a rubber raft. I shouted again before she float-
ed away.

"Was it a branch bank? Or a branch bank manager?!"

A woeful little voice answered from somewhere midst the
selenoids and oceans that separated us. " . . . a bad connection
. . . Place the call again . . ."

Then there was nothing in the earpiece. She had discon-
nected, and only the curious atonal hum of the Japanese lines
remained.

Mary had the baby in her arms. He was red as fresh beef,
screaming while plump tear globules rolled down his cheeks. I
had ignored him too long. I thought Mary would chastise me,
but she saw my worry. Her forehead clouded with the tension.

"What is it?" she whispered.

"My father's shot a bank," I said.

The winter had been like *daikon,* the peculiar Japanese
white radishes: thin, crisp, bone-like and unsustaining, yet
with enough bite to turn the common fare of days into something tolerable. I assume the winter had been likewise elsewhere, and especially in the Iroquois camp, but I do not know.

I know so little of what went on—except the established
facts, those unsatisfying instances, the lies of mere events—
that I am forced to invent some sequence. This is not so
strange. I have been forced to invent since the moment of my
slippery birth, inventing myself, my family, my place, and the
passing of time. It is my heritage, my individual Irishness.
"The indomitable Irishry," Yeats called it, but he too was a liar
by trade.

Nonetheless I will begin with the facts I know, since they
make such fine wrappings for the fabrications. The first, and
perhaps the hardest fact, for my father, was that the sixty-
three days of summer passed and Black Peggy did not leave
for her convent again. I understand, from a variety of sources
and from passionate disavowals by The Prince, that her deci-

sion to remain was a sudden one, and as much a matter of problems within her own family as problems within ours.

I imagine Old Snake on the appointed day. Rising late, with a feeling, if not that actuality, of having slept well. He must have already noticed an increase in health on my mother's sleeping countenance beside him. Little would it have mattered that she generally increases in health through the summers and declines through the autumn and deep into winter; he would have been certain that a great distress had already begun leaving her.

I am certain he went out onto the porch that day to have his coffee and to try to coax the sun to bring strength to his withering limbs. Perhaps a young boy rode by on his bicycle (or, if the hour was as early as I think, the paper boy passed), tucking away in his boyish intelligence the odd fact which The Prince had noted, that old men grow into mornings. My father might even have waved to the boy, he would have been that eager to communicate with someone, would have been fighting the urge to wake my mother, Jimmy, Deidre, everybody! (perhaps even Black Peggy herself), to get the day underway.

Surely it became afternoon around him, the shadows creeping up across the curb, over the lawn, onto the porch, and across his face, as people came and went without him, Black Peggy among them. He would have been bewildered, even angry, but never would he have broken the silence.

The fact is, by all appearances, he took it well. He didn't say a thing about it to anyone, as far as anyone can remember or cares to tell. Mary and I knew nothing at all about it until the Thanksgiving call, when someone mentioned Peggy, and I said, "Oh, she's home," and they said, "No, she never went. Didn't we tell you?"

Thanksgiving itself is among the facts, for Deidre and Black Peggy took it upon themselves as the sole unattached women to prepare the feast. My father would have scowled at this delicate alliance, for surely he still counted on Deidre to undo what had not yet been done—Deidre who attended Cambridge to learn the language of the Cabot gentry for us, so that we could reassert our claim to what was ours. Instead they functioned as concelebrant priestesses at the communion.

I feel that they must have laughed together a great deal, and combined to drive Jimmy from the kitchen. This would have rankled my father, who would have sat, as usual, at his place in the kitchen throughout the proceedings, vacating his chair only to take sleep against the pain.

Clearly he did nap, or how else would he have remained ignorant of the pudding? The pudding was an event, the one certifiable anecdote to emerge from this particular harvest feast. For Deidre had decided, with my mother's acquiescence, to plan a menu along historical lines, somewhat duplicating a typical Pilgrim feast (the turkey, inauthentic bird, being a given exception). Among the items on this menu, besides a confiture of rhubarb, apples, and raisins, was a corn pudding, which Deidre delegated to Black Peggy. By all accounts this pudding was the star of this somewhat quaint feast, a rich and heady thing, steamed to moist perfection, rich with drippings.

My father bit into a slice. He smiled.

"Well," he said, expansively, "at least there's one proper Irish dish with all this English mush!"

Witnesses report that he said it with good cheer, and directed the remark to Deidre, apparently thinking she was responsible.

"I'm pleased that you like the pudding," Deidre said, "but thank Peggy for it. The mush is my contribution."

Pat supposedly whispered into Brendan's ear odds on Deidre's storming out, causing a modest choking fit (it will be noted that we Doyles choke regularly; my mother says that Pop and my father's brothers also had "small throats," but Pat thinks we are ashamed of eating and choke to punish ourselves).

"And it's as English as can be," Deidre added. "In fact, it's the most English thing here."

Her tone must have been wonderfully crisp and condescending, since Jimmy did report to me that the menu had been so thoroughly researched that he felt like he was eating pages from a textbook, sauteed in ink.

"I wouldn't doubt that Peg could do that," my father said. He had developed a habit of calling her Peg or Meg, probably to annoy my mother.

The atmosphere around the table had become increasingly chilly. My father compounded it by speaking courtly, thus disappointing both Deidre's expectations and my mother's ability to fault him for his stolidness.

"Congratulations, Meg, my girl," my father reportedly beamed, "the Puritans were the last English with sense of self. Their Boston descendants shame them with their humorlessness."

"You wouldn't know a Puritan from a Polack, Matt," my mother said, ignoring the fact that he had thwarted her. "You sound like Pop with that hogturd talk."

"Speak for yourself, John Smithski," my father joked.

It was a terrible joke and thus guaranteed to convulse The Prince. The Prince's laughter spread to Pat and Miranda, and then to Brendan, in turn. My father had the boys with him, it may have been his last great moment of the year.

Deidre chose this unfortunate instant to make one of her uncharacteristic absent-minded remarks.

"Boston's actually quite a humorous city," she muttered.

"A funny thing happened to me on the way to Bunker Hill . . ." Brendan blurted.

The three boys plus Miranda, and my father laughed.

"You know those redcoats are a funny bunch. Take General Hooker . . . please!"

Pat's line met with similarly stupid laughter.

"You think the redcoats are funny, you should see the Red Sox," Jimmy said.

"Pilgrim Yastremski!" someone added.

Matt Doyle and his boys carried on, until even Miranda stopped laughing. One by one the women at the table lit their cheroots and went to winnowing in their icy silence; Black

Peggy was among them now, she had the power to unseat even the head *sachem;* none of the Drumcondra Iroquois braves noticed.

Matters had cleared considerably by the time of the phone call, later in the evening, wishing us a good holiday. Much of the table-talk and joking was recounted to us then. My mother's summary was that it had all been meant to be good fun, but that my father had—to put it mildly—goofed. Deidre and Peggy were hurt. That is, the boys had already been absolved of their complicity—at least within the family stories—while my father remained deposed. More importantly, Black Peggy had another solid grip on the hand-holds of family status. The story could end here, if my father hadn't shot the bank.

For I imagine that it was after this holiday feast that he began to exile himself to the darkroom, an activity that continued all winter. Ostensibly he had taken on a retirement project with a two-fold objective: first, working on the genealogy, and second, making a catalogue of all the old photographs and negatives, printing up any of the latter which had not been printed. It should become obvious that this two-fold project had but one thrust: the preservation of past glory; and, further, that the whole activity was somehow funereal.

Somehow, however, the image that comes to mind is less the burial monument and more the hive in winter; not only because the hive captures the sad, drone-like quality of my father's days in that season, but because it offers a comfortable way to understand my mother's decline into winter; a winter which was not only historically one of the worst for Buffalo and vicinity, but also one of the worst for my mother, who spent much of it in her queenly chamber, literally sick to death with colds, fevers, flus, and bronchitis.

Yet the hive is too comfortable an image. It was a sad time. My mother's ailments were complicated by the fact that Moira's children took a turn for the worse; that the snow, when it came in the middle of the glass-clear day in January, did not stop until early March, when it melted away like a bad dream; and, finally, that my mother ached for my father as much as herself. His retreat into the darkroom hurt her, for she worried that the many parting ceremonies of his, which she scrupulously mocked, might one day make sense.

Not even Jimmy's remarkable renaissance seemed to help. The Prince, removed from the burden of his own future, had settled down in school, transforming the horrendous record of his junior year into straight A's in his senior year. He began to take photographs for the school yearbook (the only one among us to follow my father's art); he played sports; he did volunteer work as part of a civics project, working with a trade-union political action committee, and staying with it after the project ended. In short, he became a proper twerp. Black Peggy watched television for hours alone at night in our living room while Jimmy was off doing constructive things, preparing for a life as a Boddhisatva for the common man.

Old Snake was too far gone to make sense of this. When my mother lapsed further and further, despite Jimmy's reformation, it seemed proof positive that Black Peggy was the canker. I imagine that sometimes as he sat in the darkroom, poring over the complicated side-branches of the genealogy of aunts from County Kerry, my father must have felt Peggy's presence below him: sprawling like a larva—a pupa—on the living room carpet, ultraviolet waves from the television screen feeding her dark eyes. She must have grown and grown in his consciousness, a sickness compressing the house.

Jimmy's unionism and his interest in photography cannot have helped either; if anything, they must have seemed to Old Snake further evidences of a helpless retracing of a worn circular path. Jimmy must have seemed determined to make his father's fate his own.

Living in the darkroom, deciphering and charting the bloodlines of ghosts, viewing the transposed images (white for dark, dark for light) of the negatives of what mostly *were* ghosts, did not help Old Snake balance things. The darkroom had been the bedroom and deathbed of my mother's one-legged father, a canny and imaginative German who had roused himself from his death stupor long enough to drink a last beer (his first liquid in days) and smoke a pipe before dying. My father took it over after years during which it had served only to store things which no one had the gumption or energy to throw out—years also during which Jimmy and Brendan, who slept next door, swore regularly that they heard the old man's ghostly crutch in the night. It was the perfect place for exile, a room which had removed itself from the house as surely as if it had been a dirigible only briefly moored there.

The snow kept coming, some nights falling for hours in the thick flakes that seem black as they fall into the light. My mother grew weaker and weaker, often dreaming of a boat, a narrow canoe which she miraculously fit within, and in which she sailed away. Black Peggy spent more and more time at our house, sometimes staying all night on the living room sofa (and perhaps elsewhere in the house), blanketed in only the pale silk fabric of light from the empty screen. First Christmas, then New Year's, Valentine's, and President's Day came and went, holidays of decreasing reality.

On St. Patrick's Day the court kids caught The Stranger.

There is a Sutra of Past Causes and Present Effects, which is the story of the Buddha, Shaku. It brings comfort in a world of things and is useful.

After Colleen had placed her call again and the sad facts of the unfortunate assault of the bank branch were known (and related to Mary), Mary put the boy to bed and then did not return to the room. I sat by the charcoal brazier, trying to make some sense of it all, seeking the relation between past causes and present effects.

There is none. And yet I could not get my mind away from trying to conceive how my father deluded himself enough to think that the bosses had once nearly fallen from neglect, that the family (as an idea? a reality?) had nearly brought the working man to liberation. How, I wondered, could he have thought so through the Thirties, the War, the proliferation of things that followed. My meditation was made more difficult by the fact that I honestly have no sense of history as it is commonly understood. I have absolutely no idea how it felt to walk on an April day in 1938; whether one imagined that change would come as it did; if one's clothing felt as awkward as it appears in one of the ghost photographs my father has carefully printed from forlorn negatives. Less still do I understand whether someone walking on that April day would have been aware of the ferment in governments, or of the arguments among certain Bohemian intellectuals of the New York left-wing concerning the nature and future of socialism. Or even the more pragmatic discussions of union organizers in Detroit.

Could he have thought then, returning home from having met my mother, a sassy, black-haired girl who flirted with his brother but ignored his own awkward silences and stammering jokes, that he was about to work a quiet revolution? That the dreams of a proletariat, a word he surely could not use comfortably in a conversation, if at all, were by all stars within the grasp of his personal history?

I was too stupid to be able to make sense of these questions, and I am still. I left off my meditation and listened to the wind, the moaning woman. It was cold, despite the charcoals which leered orange through the ventilator holes. Winter in our district is drafts, moist silent eels. A monk once told me that winter is when it is worst to meditate, that the drafts seem to enter the hollows of the bones, whistling through the silence. He had pushed the saffron sleeve back from his wrist; its bony, ivory sheen looked like a wind instrument. He smiled crazily. Monks are fond of that, jokes upon themselves and all creation.

I went out into the garden, hoping the cold would wake me, hoping the open air would give me something to see. You can see nothing in our part of the country, only fire flies on summer nights. In winter there is nothing but shadows of shadows. The occasional dustings of snow, therefore, can sometimes blind a man for days.

There was no snow this night, only cold. The Japanese are

crazy for snow, they will go hundreds of miles to see it or slide down upon it with skis. They reminded me in this way of San Franciscans, the American Buddhists. I once had occasion to spend some months there and I remember that the radio stations announced the first snow in the mountains, then days later the newspapers had stories about the hundreds of automobiles which had crawled up into those same mountains, bogging down upon, or sliding from, treacherous narrow roads. The approach highways were bumper to bumper with paralyzed machines, and the stories warned people not to see the snow anymore.

I looked for snow that night in the garden, sometimes squinting so hard that I saw blurs of what might have been orange and neon-green flakes. Each time the shadows returned. The only reality was the snorting of the far off horses. Finally I was chilled through and I had to go in and sleep.

But then I experienced satori.

Satori has come cheap in recent years. It is one of the readily misunderstood foreign phenomenon that a culture like ours can latch onto. So its element of mystery—its genuine inexpressibleness—is made to order for America, where it can be easily translatable as lack of definition. Satori becomes style.

For several reasons therefore, I have distrusted the whole notion. What little I do trust about it has to do with its general uselessness, part of the wondrous cleansing pessimism of all Buddhism. *Zap! You know. Zap! No.*

I do understand, however, the predisposition, the emptiness, which usually accompanies satori (and which makes it an impossible chore for most Americans, except for the few tribes of us who live on the outskirts and are not fooled by what crowds us). The chill, and the shadows, had brought the emptiness to me without my knowing. As I came back into the house, fitting the double screens behind me, even my lungs seemed empty, bereft of either air or fluid.

But now (at exactly the point where I should be able to tell it) there is nothing really to say.

I undressed in the dark and lay down on the mats next to

Mary, fitting our bodies together, placing the comforter squarely over us. I felt rich then. I felt that her warmth was the greatest pleasure I could ever have. Had ever had. There was a rightness to it.

I had accomplished my meditation about my father when it least seemed I could. I understood what Jimmy meant to do with his life. I understood my own life. I even knew why my father would claim that we Doyles were descended from Irish kings.

For a warm man is a rich man in the winter.

The court kids vigilante activities had brought no success, other than the fortuitous capture and inquisition of a commonplace flasher who had been unfortunate enough to attempt his routine in the presence of one of the wee girls. According to Jimmy, there was a momentary elation when the wee girl screamed, alerting her stake-out team, for the street was dark enough that the squad of them thought they had discovered The Stranger himself. But when they brought the whimpering fellow into the light, it turned out to be only Weird Joey, a mildly retarded young man, well known in the neighborhood for his habit of juggling screwdrivers for hours on end on his front porch.

Weird Joey, as it turned out, was not very successful as a flasher, since he restricted his exposure to baring his undershorts. Or at least the outer of the two pair he wore. Nonetheless, the court kids tied him to a tree near the courts and interrogated him for hours. The Prince left in disgust that night.

"Everytime they asked a question about The Stranger, Weird Joey cried. He thought they were going to strangle him," Jimmy explained.

After the ordeal, however, the court kids redeemed themselves in Jimmy's eyes.

"They made him a court kid," Jimmy said proudly. "They rehabilitated him by telling him he could hang out with us.

Between games he insists on polishing the basketball with a cloth."

Although "struck" is not exactly the correct word for The Stranger's appearances, he did strike at least twice more through the summer and fall. During his second appearance—to the Mendola's younger sister, Bee—The Stranger made it known that he was aware of the stake-outs. He asked her why her brothers feared the truth about their lives. He told her to tell them that they could not escape the meaninglessness before them, even if he were captured. More importantly, and dramatically, he left a first-class relic with her, a genuine momento or a clue, depending on how one views it.

It seems that Bee had trouble repeating the message that The Stranger wanted her to give to her brothers and their friends; she kept forgetting or blocking-out the word "meaninglessness" (she is only seven). After he had tried to help her remember the word once or twice, he reached into his pocket and pulled out a notebook, then handed her a page.

It was a common lined notebook page, like the kind my father uses to write down the cumulative records of sports teams as well as the exposure times for the negatives which he has printed. This page, however, had a carefully cut square of newspaper pasted to it: *Meaninglessness*, it said. The Stranger had been prepared; or he kept a notebook of critical concepts.

These facts I learned from The Chief, my brother Pat, who had been brought in on the investigation as a consultant because he reads more newspapers and magazines than most anybody on earth. The court kids had hoped that The Chief would be able to identify the newspaper from which the word had been cut.

Their choice of Pat as consultant was fitting, not only because he cannot resist subscribing to any new or older publication emanating from fringe constituencies, but also because— on any given day—perhaps ninety percent of these publications would have printed a headline including the word. The Chief reads periodicals in the way that doctors read cardiograms; he is interested in the process of decline.

"Hell," he told me on the phone, "I had already located

three instances from this month alone, before they brought the thing to me. With enough time, I could of found hundreds."

The fact that Pat had looked through current issues was an indicator of his interest. He almost always reads chronologically, sliding a paper or magazine from the bottom of one of the two six foot stacks of unstable printed matter which he keeps next to his desk. (Once my sister Moira house-sat for Pat and Miranda and, wishing to do them an added service, she had a junkman haul away both of The Chief's pillars of paper. He mourned them for a year, much of which he spent in the periodical rooms of area libraries, trying to catch up. Fortunately Moira had not cleaned out the walk-in closet full of popular pornographic magazines, which Pat calls his "Imago Mundi Collection.")

Pat was disappointed, he hadn't had to look far to identify The Stranger's source. "It was *The New York Times*," he said. "The Prince should have known. Any fool could see that . . ."

For awhile, apparently, the court kids had considered writing to *The Times* and asking for a list of subscribers from the neighborhood.

"I pointed out that it's on sale at the drugstore," Pat said, "and that *The Times* probably doesn't recognize vigilante subpoenas."

Through late fall and winter, there were no reported contacts with The Stranger. It was fortunate, since the court kids were driven inward, reduced to their cold weather routine of visiting from house to house, hitchhiking to the shopping mall, and meeting at pizzarias. Then good fortune came their way in the form of tragedy. Cunningham's mother died on Christmas Eve, walking back from mass. After an appropriate mourning period (one which Jimmy took very hard), Cunningham's older sister, who had been left both the house and the care of her brother (their father gone for six years by then), moved out to live with her boyfriend, making only nightly visits to the house to prepare supper for the boy who lived alone.

The court kids thus had a clubhouse. But their parents, Old

Snake especially, had great fears, with at least half the group forbidden to even associate with Cunningham any longer.

Cunningham must have felt like a general in exile. The house which he all but inherited was one of those houses which at some point in their existence simply quit living. First the siding begins to chip in small blisters, hundreds commemorating each winter day's frost, each summer day's scorching. Then hardware, like railings and gutters, begins to sag and wobble from the rot in the wood around them. Slowly the chipping gives way to whole sheets of flaking paint, and the hardware lets loose and disappears. Floating away. These events had already taken place in the years between the deaths of Mr. and Mrs. Cunningham. The original stain, or what little of it had seeped into the grain of the wood siding, was all that remained of color, and that too had been grey, only slightly brighter than the grey in those places where the bare wood had bleached with the seasons.

Windows in our immediate neighborhood are an especial curse, since many of the houses were built with casings salvaged from the temporary structures of the Pan-American Exposition where President McKinley was shot, and thus nearly everyone had odd-sized windows. The more affluent neighbors have had aluminum combination windows installed, and these flat silver rims appear like a pox on the angular houses. Less wealthy residents suffer the necessity of continual caulking and wood-puttying in the places where the windows had been forced into place by carpenters working from stubborn instinct or mail-order designs. The poorest neighbors, like the Cunninghams, gradually allow the light to diminish, filling the openings with plywood sheeting like merchants do after an arson. The constant light of television sets compensates for the diminishment.

Cunningham, then, lived like an old Irish Da, his daughterly sister looking in on him at regular intervals, but otherwise left alone to find what light he could until the last light came. For a time he certainly must have consoled himself with what cannabis he could afford, also with revelling, and with beer from the cans with which he eventually constructed a room divider; but these pleasures must have paled as the loneliness increased, especially since most of the kids had deserted him, a number of them surely quite pleased that their parents' injunctions had saved them from the necessity of spending time at this dim house. Cunningham had grown too old, but had done at a much faster rate than the most of them, who would also grow too old too soon.

He too grew old into mornings. He was afraid at night, according to Jimmy, and used to go to bed immediately when his sister left, unless some of the court kids came to visit. He would rise at dawn and walk the streets, stopping somewhere along the way to buy a Coke for breakfast.

The chief visitors were Black Peggy and Jimmy, with Peggy there more often. Since she was already spending so much of her time alone with the television, she began, once Christmas had passed, to spend hours at Cunningham's rather than my parents. There appears to have been no question of loyalties, since Jimmy often accompanied her, using a room at Cunningham's as a study, but also since Peggy looked upon Cunningham as another child to mother.

Peggy retreated to the house with a vengeance, going there like Ameratsu had gone to her cave, removing all light from the world until the *kami* lured her out again with music and dancing. In her own way Peggy, like the goddess, mourned the loss of love in the world; Jimmy served as her guardian and sometime disciple, although the ways of the *kami*, music and dancing, were not his ways.

Yet Jimmy's retreat did not affect his newfound sense of achievement. If anything, it spurred him on. It was as if he felt that the surest recognition of the *sunyata*, the emptiness, was to succeed in the outward world. The Prince was slowly becoming his own sort of Buddhist, building his own eightfold way.

Old Snake understood little, if anything, of all this, if my guess is correct. What he was able to see was that Jimmy had been doing very well and now he was spending time at Cunningham's instead of either at his studies and activities or in the darkroom. This despair was compounded by a geometric progression in the same logic which had led to my father's identification of Black Peggy as a tool of the corporate classes. For, although he was forced both by disposition and by pragmatic realities to be sympathetic to the Cunningham boy whenever the matter came up for talk; Old Snake did not miss an opportunity to point out that the boy's orphaning by his older sister had resulted because she (*too*—although he dare not say so directly) was one of the pleasure-seeking, man-blinding products of American corporate life.

In his wildest and worse logics, he would turn Deidre scarlet with rage.

"All this talk about how commercials make them sex objects," he might say. "Nobody mentions that TV is where they go to school. Today's girls learn from those things. They learn to lure, and not to have families. Bankers dance! And the car companies reward hussies with opera windows and upholstery to match their dresses."

"Who is this them?" Deidre would seethe at him. "I am one of them."

"That's not the point," he'd say. "Don't ever say that."

"You're crazy," she'd say. "What are you talking about?"

"Meg's sandals, for example," Old Snake would speak unctuously, knowing he could gall Deidre, "now mind, I really like Meg, but shoes are shoes! Sandals are not for winters."

"Her name is Peggy," Deidre might manage to sputter.

"Right, Peg!"

But Deidre would be gone, unable to receive his profound smile.

Deidre should probably have stayed in her Cambridge rooms, but my mother kept getting sicknesses upon sicknesses, and Deidre came home nearly every weekend. The house was left to her, and Peggy and The Prince, from day to day. The Buddha spent as little time as he could at home, for he alternated between muttering threats to punch the old man out and falling to weeping fits at the unfairness of it all. Pat stayed clear, most likely readying his funerary pinstripe suit.

138

The married sisters came by when they could, but my mother didn't like them to, not wanting to think that she was as sick as she was, or that she was disrupting others' families.

Old Snake complicated things because his own fears were so transparent: he worried that she would die, and since he could not control that, he controlled what he could. He would come down from the darkroom, having breathed too much of the fumes of ghosts, not feeling at all well himself, and stir up a fight.

Peggy was good with him, because of her nature; and Jimmy had seen something and so he was placid with my father. This left the burden of rage to Deidre, who did not want to hurt him because she, too, knew he was afraid.

Those few court kids who were allowed to visit the Cunningham house had begun a project, organized by Jim, to help Cunningham repaint and patch the interior plaster and do whatever odd things that would help bring some light there.

"Pride of ownership and all that," Jimmy later explained. "It was terribly middle-class, but that is the only life he can possibly have . . ."

Then one day my father forbade Jimmy to go to the Cunningham's whenever the sister was likely to be there. It was the first time in years that household observers could remember him forbidding anything.

They were all—Deidre included—at the table when he made his ruling. My mother had managed to come downstairs for the first time in three days or more; and he put the injunction in the form of a comment to her. About her.

"I don't think your mother likes your going to Cunningham's when that girl's around. I wish you wouldn't."

My mother puffed a cigarette and watched him with weary eyes. She was too weak to answer, too worried about his worry about her.

"Why?" It was Deidre who asked, she had gone to Cunningham's a few times with Peggy and Jimmy.

"Because she's not the right type," he said. "She left that house empty."

139

His complaint was a smokescreen; he meant he did not want to be alone at home.

"But his sister is his family, Mr. Doyle," Peggy said. "It would be like we were rejecting that."

"His family left him! *You* wouldn't be able to see that," my father said.

It was a slip into accusation. Unpolitic and bitter, he had slapped Black Peggy with a remark. Deidre did not rush upstairs this time. Instead she calmly walked to the hall and put her coat on, then reappeared in the kitchen.

"I'm going over to help the Cunningham girl get dinner for her brother," she said.

Deidre had not meant to be cruel. When she left the house, Old Snake began to sob, dry like a horse. Peggy and my mother sobbed with him.

My mother's crying brought on an attack of bronchial coughing. It stopped my father's tears. During those days he watched her as if she would not return from any fit of coughing, watching like someone watches the thin wake of a canoe moving away.

The coughing lapsed and my mother confronted him.

"Matt, that girl was kept under her mother's thumb. She would have been married long ago."

"It's still not right to leave that kid alone," he insisted, but sadly, without intensity.

"No," she said, looking him directly, "it isn't, is it?"

His obstinancy failed. She wouldn't have wanted to do that, to drain him of the last, unreasonable resistance.

"Go on," he muttered from his silence, gesturing wearily to Peggy and Jim. "Go on . . ." He went up to the darkroom.

But they didn't yet. My mother sat quietly for awhile, her bleared eyes fixed on some middle distance. When she is tired like this, my mother's eyes are coals, dark and separate, set off by the puff of flesh around them. Between drags of her cigarette, she bit at her thick thumb to ward off tears, to keep from coughing again.

I invent these things, but I have seen them before. And The

Prince watched her carefully that night, knowing she was not aware then of who watched her, nor of anything outside the private space she gazed in.

She woke from this gaze like an old woman after a nap, irritable, somewhat bitter, but elated nonetheless in a sad, tired way.

"Go on," she said to them, but she did not let them go yet.

"He's right, you know," she said. "There are no more families. Edmund's is the last one, and I'm not sure of him."

Jimmy knew enough to know that he was supposed to remember this, to tell me what she had said about me.

"There are other ways," she said. "Cunningham's sister could have moved into the big house with her boyfriend. But they all want their own . . ."

She sighed hugely.

"Who can blame her?" she asked. "I'd do the same . . ."

Then she recovered herself.

"Go on!" she snapped. "Haven't you two caused enough trouble?"

The standard way to the Cunningham house was to vault the fence in the backyard of the funeral parlor on Seneca Street and come through the backyard. Someone who observed the court kids carefully, like The Stranger, should have known this. But that March night when Billy Leary came around the double garage of the mortician's livery and approached the cyclone fence, he could see the man in the long overcoat clearly, peering through the back window into Cunningham's dining room. The undertaker's yard light did not shine enough toward Cunningham's house for Billy Leary to identify the figure at the window, but it gave enough light that Billy knew they had him. He slipped back home and called the house to let them know. With the confusion of the St. Paddy's Day party it was simple enough for the kids to pass the word without notice. A few of them slipped out the front door and went around the block to rendezvous with Billy for the rush from the undertaker's side. The rest of them waited within the house for the chime of St. John's clock, which, in the best traditions of television drama, would be their signal to come toward him from both sides.

Cunningham and the other kid, my brother Jim, were the first to reach the man at the window, for they leaped from the backporch on the first chime of the clock, pushing The Stranger face-first into the old and dark snow of the back yard.

Jimmy, therefore, was the first to know that the man was his and my father.

chapter seven

on the nature of things

It is as certain as death that Matthew Doyle was not The Stranger. Although, as I sit in the night on the porch and think of what it is I could say to him, I think it would be a start to ask him. To have him tell me what he was or was not.

But the wind has shifted and the jet airplanes have begun to take the final approach which takes them low and roaring over our neighborhood, so low that you can smell the fumes of their engines, spy the silver fuselages in whatever moonlight there is. The noise is too much for questions. Even when the planes do not come for awhile, when they do not coast the city and drop low over this narrow village in the last turn before they disgorge business men from Chicago, Boston, and New York, or returning vacationers from kindlier climes; between them there is the sound of laughter from the open windows of this spring night. The laughing comes from all the houses around us as well as our own, escaping like canaries into the night.

Surely none of the court kids thought him The Stranger—

that is, with the two great exceptions of the one who argued that justice must proceed from the evidence of appearances, and the other who insisted that things are as they are.

Lord knows, the question has been debated often enough in each of the days since, up to and past the trial a few days ago. News creeps through a neighborhood like ours. In each of the houses where light and noise now flee to the street in the lull between airplanes, doubtless someone discussed my father's probable guilt.

Yet there are reasons enough, enough occasions where it was impossible that it could have been him, to dismiss the question with certainty. Always however there is the fact that in the days since—as you would expect of one so wily as The Stranger—he has not appeared again.

It is troubling to know that no one will know, not even if I were to ask him. I won't ask. It is one of those questions which betray the questioner, and one for which no answer will ever suffice. Should The Stranger appear again tomorrow, in the light of a May morning with my father safely under house arrest and before witnesses, our age is so drunk with imitation that the worst skeptics would remain unconvinced of his past innocence, thinking the real Stranger an impostor.

Both those who know me least and those who know me best accuse me of thinking too much about things, of trying to understand too much of an incomprehensible world: to discover each personal characteristic, every element of setting, even to the point of trying to spell out the motivations behind each of the most trivial actions, the most aimless of remarks. I suppose it is true. My mother says I have always been "a picky one."

But what those who know me least do not know is that *I know* that eventually the surface of meaningfulness fails. Only then are we ready to be moved by events. Life, or what I suppose we are given to know of it, is the miraculous event which tumbles all understanding, like a weed flowering through concrete.

Even so, given this knowledge, I nonetheless curse and wish bad cess upon the stinking protty soil that brought my father so sadly to bloom.

My father was hurt. The ambush had succeeded entirely, and the weight of Cunningham and Jim upon him had wrenched his already skewed vertebrae. He moaned in the snow, nearly unconscious with the pain, and the boys' first reaction was terror for his life. They were certain they had killed him. Thus, when the flanking platoon of Billy Leary and the other court kids scaled the fence and pincered in on the unfortunate Stranger, whooping and singing, Jimmy and Cunningham reacted in panic. Apparently their first instinct was to scream at the others, calling them off, but their shouts of protest only mingled with the Iroquois whoops of the others.

Cunningham decked Billy Leary with a single, unexpected punch. The other court kids silenced instantly, and now there were two victims: Matt Doyle moaning in the snow, and Billy Leary unconscious and bleeding torrents against the foundation where his head had hit.

"Good work," a caustic voice pronounced from the back porch. It was Black Peggy, viewing the carnage.

The court kids stood like rural louts at a barn fight.

"Bring them inside!" Peggy ordered. "Mr. Doyle first. The snow will be good for Billy's skull."

In retrospect it is clear that the eventual disposition of my father's case had been decided then. The court kids had established their kingdom and dealt their justice, but when it was necessary to take responsibility for what they had done, they stood with their balls in their pockets. Peggy acted. She was the *Sean Bhean Bhoct*, the poor old woman of Ireland, left to clean up the leavings of the strapping lads. But because she did not actually decide then, because they were let to bring in the prisoner and the wounded, there were many hours to pass before the boys themselves would understand this.

And so my father was left to suffer both a delirium of pain and the agony of hearing his case tried before them, as he lay in the downstairs bedroom. I am certain that he conceived his crime against Peggy and Holy Waspdom in this time, and that it was only a matter of retrieving his relative health from where he had left it in the snow which kept him from acting much sooner.

It turns out that his back itself had escaped the punishment of the assault. He had bruised his hip bone, strained his back muscles, and certainly compressed the already weak jelly of his backbones, but the bones escaped dislocation or breakage. But they did not know this that night, and so they were careful in bringing him in. One of the court kids, an unrepentant boy scout, assumed the medic's role, directing the rest in the construction of a makeshift stretcher, using a blanket and two tent poles. Upon the insistence of the scout, they left my father where he had been dropped while they did this work. The result was that the worst of his injuries was a nasty patch of frostbite on the back of his neck, where snow had stuffed itself under his collar. The crescent kiss of white remained un-noticed all night, and has since took its place among the pale scars and bleached pocks of the rest of his scald-colored neck. It burns, however, at the merest hint of chill, a continual reminder of his shame.

Once they had him inside, the scout insisted on offering a joint to my father, arguing that its anesthetic properties would calm whatever wrath my father could summon. The sugges-tion was met with less wrath than a howl of increasing shame.

"You think because you kicked my ass it makes me one of you outlaws?" my father shouted.

"How about whiskey?" the scout asked.

"My god, yes. That, or a ride home to my bed," my father retorted.

It is curious, and grist for the mill, that my father did not press his advantage at this point. Knowing our neighborhood village, observers note that all my father needed to do was muster whatever authority and outrage he could. Insisting upon his god-given rights to check into his children's activi-ties, and proclaiming his innocence, he could have had them quaking then, with a ride home to follow and none of this nonsense about The Stranger. Instead he accepted the pint square bottle of Southern Comfort, "stinking stuff," as he blurted once in coming days, and lay back and accepted his pain and growled at his fate.

To be sure, in the hours of the argumentation that followed, such a grave cultural lapse, and damning instance, did not go unnoticed.

"He could have said he wasn't him," one of the wee girls had reportedly ventured. "I mean when we brought him in."

"He didn't know we even thought he was him," Cunningham defended.

"He was caught," Jimmy said.

"Crap," Peggy answered, "he wasn't doing anything he thought of being caught at. The Stranger never does."

My father, for his part, only moaned, and by this time of night the moans were losing their force.

As best as I can reconstruct things, the whole of the evening's proceedings took this form. Cunningham, whether oddly or no, took the part of the defense all night. The two great exceptions aforementioned, Peggy and Jim, prosecuted from different flanks: Jimmy argued strictly from appearances, although possibly also from misplaced guilt, that the man at the window had been doing what The Stranger does and therefore was The Stranger, however sad that seemed; Peggy did not deny the facts but rather the sadness of it.

"What did you expect," she reportedly said again and again, "someone from out of town? Some kind of real Stranger? When you start hunting among yourselves, you expect to find yourselves."

Although the wisdom of this view was too fine a thread to clothe them without repeated weaving, it eventually won the day, or rather the night; but not without real argument and, eventually, a chastening and gloomy awareness as they tried the garment of guilt for size. The Stranger was one of them, and so no stranger, and they would have to protect this secret and Mr. Doyle, who they otherwise (and confusingly) knew was not The Stranger. The hunt was over; the hunt was continual; they left quietly that night, sober and older. And my father, of course, was helpless in mounting any future defense: for they all knew he was not guilty, but they all accepted that he was The Stranger. This artifice of Peggy's smouldered against him; what she had woven was a straitjacket for him. Was truth of a sort.

But, if the night ended in disillusioned silence, it began with buoyant anticipation and cockeyed glee. They had done something wrong, they all knew, and there was a certain exhilaration. Likewise, they would have to do something quite correct and wondrously mature, for the father of one of them lay hurt and in ambiguous disgrace among them and had to be helped and judged both. The maturity and immediate reality of these facts brought its own exhilaration.

First, however, there was panic. Wee girls wept like keeners at a wake, weeping both out of pure anxiety, and because they did not know what else to do. Billy Leary had, in the excitement, awakened from his wounded slumber and walked off, leaving an intermittent trail of blood and footsteps. My father, early in his ordeal, had energy enough to bray commands and mutter useless threats in his moaning. Besides, most every one of the court kids was drunk with beer and Southern Comfort, and made hysterical by dope of dubious quality.

The Prince remembers the sequence of the beginning. They had just brought my father into the downstairs bedroom, and the medic was attending him. The kids who had gone after Billy Leary came running in.

"He's gone! He's gone!" one shouted.

A wee girl shrieked, "Oh Jesus, he's dead!" She began to weep.

"It's no miracle," Black Peggy snarled. "Billy Leary didn't ascend into heaven, I'll guarantee you."

"Up jumped Finnegan!" The Prince remembers exclaiming, but no one caught the mention. He says he remembers feeling sad and old then; that he wanted to take Dad home.

Cunningham resumed his generalship. He dispatched pairs of kids after Billy, one pair to track him through the snow, another to inquire at his house.

"Make like nothing happened, when you get to Leary's," he said, "and don't say nothing about Mr. . . . ."

"The Stranger," Peggy said calmly, overriding Cunningham's hesitancy.

For awhile, pending the news on Billy, there were no formal proceedings. Court kids talked in groups, wee girls wept and giggled. At some point one of the girls got extraordinarily hysterical.

"He'll tell my mother, he'll tell my mother, and she'll kill me," the girl chanted.

Jimmy exploded. "He will not tell your goddamn mother! Even if . . . if none of this happened, my father doesn't call people's parents. We're not a bunch of fucking bingo players at our house."

Much later, when Jim related this comment to me, I had the sense that he was waiting for me to point out the class distinction he had made. I did not disappoint him. "Well, we're not," he said, "and I never said I wanted anybody to stay that type."

The search parties returned without Billy. The tracking party had lost the trail of blood when Billy apparently headed down the center of the street. The party dispatched to Billy's house had not found him there either. When the search party showed up at Leary's door, his mother told them about the party at Cunningham's. She seemed to suspect that Billy had given her a line. The kids ran all the way back to the party. Within minutes the phone rang. Everyone knew it was the Leary's, checking Billy's story, and so they let it ring, confused about what to say. Finally, Cunningham picked up the phone, but he just held it there, unwilling to make excuses to Billy's parents. Peggy took the phone from his hands.

"Hi, Mrs. Leary. Yeah, they got here. Sure, he's here! There's a party," she waved her free hand, orchestrating appropriate party sounds, and the court kids obliged. "Well... yes, I guess you could," Peggy continued, "but frankly, Mrs. Leary, Billy's ah . . . Yes. Before he got here, I think. He was pretty drunk when he came in . . ." She had sacrificed Billy to the cause, but shut off Mrs. Leary's concern. "I will certainly make sure he does," she said. "They're walking him around now. He fell and hit his head, a little scrape." The crisis passed.

Of course, I invent all this. All Jimmy said was that Peggy handled things when the Learys called, but I know how these things would have happened, what Peggy would have said, what the others would have done. It is dismaying but, for all the extreme differences there are between Jimmy's group and my own at his age, I know the old patterns still hold. They were frightened, we have always grown up frightened here. It is what is most painful for me in watching Jim and his friends, knowing that all their raw knowledge does not balm this fright; in fact, makes them more vulnerable to it. I find myself wondering sometimes why I wish that my own son could grow with at least a sense of the fright which we all grew with, why I would want him to be heir to the medieval ambiguities of a dark tribe.

What is also dismaying and painful, however, is how vividly I can convince myself that I do not invent the occurrences of that night at all; how thoroughly I have reassembled what I can of its sequences and changes. So much so that I can readily lose track of the simple fact that I was not there. For my images I blame my own medieval ambiguities.

After the phone call, the court kids realized that Billy was not the only missing warrior. They knew that people at my parent's house would be sure to worry. Something had to be done, both immediately and in the long run.

The immediate need for resolution was left up to The Prince. He was convinced that he should call the house and ask for Dad, claiming to want a ride to another party or a pizzaria. Jim did not do this willingly. He did not want to lie. For a moment or two he argued that he should just call my mother and "break it to her."

"What?" Cunningham demanded.

"That . . . we caught The Stranger."

"Bullshit," Cunningham, admirably, responded, "we don't know that at all. You really want to hurt her like that? Even if it is so?"

150

Jimmy demurred, but to his credit the call was the last lie he told about that night. Later in the night, he called home again to say that my father had gone drinking with them (when Jim called the first time, Deidre had said that my father went out for cigarettes; he said they would try to catch him—the first and most imaginative of his slanted truths, he couldn't help laughing at his own pun, Prince that he is). Then when they returned in the early morning, Jim said that Dad had hurt himself in a fall, that it had been his fault. "I kind of surprised him," he explained, lamely.

My mother was not at all convinced of course. Even if my father had been in the habit of going out drinking with children (or going out drinking at all), she would not have believed the story. In fact, what is the single most surprising thing for me about the whole episode is that Jimmy did not understand this, does not—I think—understand still.

It should not surprise me. None of my brothers, not even the wedded Pat, understand the long intimacy and secret awareness of my parents' marriage. Pat frequently complains to me that he cannot stand (could not, even before Matt Doyle's fall) visiting with my parents because they bag at each other.

"They wound me with their barbs," he said once, "even if they are beyond pain themselves. Even if their hides are thick with constant pain. It hurts me to see them hate like this."

"It's not hate," I insisted, "you don't let yourself see how well they know each other. It's like you refuse to accept some primal awareness. You talk like you don't think they sleep together, let alone talk."

"They don't," he said, pausing, "not really."

"How the hell do you know, Lord Oedipus?"

"Do you?" he asked.

He was right, but he had missed the point. My own ignorance about my parents' relationship, on any terms, was at least a celebration of the mystery—the *intimacy*, that word again!—I granted them. I don't know why he didn't see that, why none of the three of them do, but I also don't know why I did see or do. My mother was right that time, when she talked about me for the benefit of Black Peggy and The Prince, saying there were no more families but mine, and that she wasn't sure about me.

For I am not sure either. Intimacy is either a quality I lack or something I will not recognize until it is nearly too late, for Mary or for me. I try for it, but I think I end up only stuffing cotton in the chinks of the walls and the screens, keeping out the moths of trivial activity, while outside the moon shines and inside it colors the wings of the crushed moths beneath my feet. I am an Irish-Oriental version of the little Dutchboy, saving an imaginary home town, while the real floods in.

Still, I do see that much: the comedy of my life, my resistance to the truly intimate. And so I think I see what my brothers will not, although I assume Pat will learn of its existence if he stays long enough with Miranda, just as I have learned that much from the time of my time with Mary. Jimmy, however, has hardly begun his time.

Yet Peggy knows. Just as I exempt my sisters, even mad Moira, who is intimate with her children and with lying spirits, I also necessarily exempt Peggy from the primal ignorance about my parents. For Peggy had urged Jim to lie straight through, knowing (I think) that it would make his ignorance less painful, when my mother and father eventually got the stories straight, which they would whether they actually discussed the events of that night or not.

Perhaps it was this knowing of Peggy's, as much as anything, which finally drove my father to his mad action. For the thought strikes me: just as he could not see the truth of Peggy's argument about him, just as he could not see how it could eventually prevail, could not see with her clarity that he was indeed The Stranger in one way or another; perhaps he also himself does not see, as she does, as my sisters and my mother surely do, the intimacy of his life with his wife.

After suffering the deliberations of the neighborhood children during his long night at Cunningham's, my father might have been excused if his public trial had not shaken him as much as it might have. But, as a longtime law-abiding citizen, who shook and stammered with *politesse* when in recent years he had fallen into a series of careless traffic tickets issued by fresh-faced, young cops; the reality of a trial for felony charges withered him beyond the withering of his constant pains. Never mind the fact that the lawyer, Maloney, had assured him there would be a plea-bargain—the contemporary right of even common criminals—my father still shook as he stood there in his out-of-fashion, plaid Sears suit and stiff, unaccustomed dress shoes. He even seemed to try to keep respectful distance from Maloney. The lawyer was a genial sort of courthouse hack, with longtime connections to the local Democratic organization, where, in fact, my parents had secured his services. Although they might have called him directly since they had known him for years, including his years—both in law school and after he set up his practice— when he worked in the plant, at least once under my father's indirect supervision.

Now however Maloney wore a courtroom blue suit and mail-order Brooks Brothers oxford shirt, and his fingernails shone with colorless lacquer, and his Black Irish, coal-dark hair was blown dry and razored to a fine line where the oxford collar met his workingclass flesh. And so my father and Maloney engaged in a little dance—my father moving a respectful half-step away, Maloney joining the gap in a gesture of solidarity and comfort—as they stood for the preliminary reading of charges by the Polish clerk, under the watchful gaze of the bemused and regal judge, a black man, who like the clerk and Maloney owed his presence there to what my father did not share in: the regular and understandable functioning of the governance and customs of the Democratic party of Erie County, in cooperation with the banks, factories, churches, social agencies, service organizations, and opposition party of said same county and the whole of capitalistic culture.

It made for a comic dance, the conjunction of these forces

and my father. And the judge—a moon-faced man, whose skin seemed to have a dusting of talcum over it, except for the forehead which unaccountably was beaded with cool and silvery drops of perspiration—can be forgiven for the fact that he seemed to enjoy the comedy too much, and was barely able to compress the laughter, which nonetheless showed in his walnut wide eyes. A few others, pimps in the pews and a car-thief or two, did not suppress their laughter; although the hookers in the courtroom, and all of my family, including my brothers, maintained an admirable dignity.

We were all there, except for Moira who had a weeping fit at the last moment before entering the courtroom and was banished by my mother; and we all tried to avoid watching my father shuffle with Maloney before the black judge.

I wish I could say my father always was brave then, but it is too much to want one's father always to be brave. The laughter in the room especially seemed to frighten him, and he stopped dancing and glanced back over his shoulder to us with a woeful look that seemed to acknowledge his realization that, in acting to save his dignity, he had foolishly lost it.

I say he looked at us, but I know he looked to my mother. For the woeful expression was soon followed by a subterranean smile and a relaxation of his whole face and body, which made me wish I had stolen a look at whatever moment of passion and compassion passed between their eyes.

Looking down the row of us, I saw face after face contorted and wet with tears: Pat, Miranda, Brendan, Colleen, Sally and Harry, Deidre, Jimmy, and Peggy, each seemed proud of him—the tears were proud tears—how tall and handsome he was there in his grey suit and now with a silly smile. Only my mother's face was not marked with tear streaks. Although her flesh was also soft with pride and love, her eyes were defiantly black and noble. Our faces contorted because we dare not cry in the face of her defiance, because we feared that she would banish us with Moira.

I knew then that none of my father's agonies that night at Cunningham's, or even in the detainment cell at the police precinct later in the month, had equalled his discomfort at forcing my mother to make her private defiance public. Not even when Billy Leary had returned that night—drunk with the sixpacks he had consumed against his hurt, and shouting that my father should be put in jail for punching him—had my father been so shamed.

By the time Billy had returned, Black Peggy had prevailed. She shut Billy up and went in to explain to my father, with Jimmy lurking at the door jamb. My father was dozing on and off, but he interrupted Peggy when she began to summarize the discussions.

"I heard it all," he said briskly, then yawned. "Or all I want to hear."

Then he raised his voice to her—Jimmy feared before the trial that he would have to testify that he had witnessed a threat, for Peggy swore she remembered none of it—and he raised himself partially from the bed.

"I know your kind, young lady, and we'll have it out one day soon. I promise you that. I'll make them see you for what you are, I swear. I didn't work forty some odd goddamn years in the plant for nothing."

These words I am sure of, not only because I made The Prince recite them to me several times, but also because I checked them once with my father, when I arrived in town, a few days before the trial.

"You're damn right, that's what I said," he said.

"What did you mean? Were you going to shoot her? Or was the bank the point?"

"You know what I said, and you have a brain," he said. "It's none of your damn business otherwise. You weren't born a professor; you were a steelworker's kid. You figure it out."

He refused to say anything more about it then, and my mother arrived on the porch within minutes of our brief exchange. It was as if she were saving him from any trials but the public one, and he was not able to settle anywhere in the house during those days—or from what my brothers say, in the days before—without her arriving there to protect him. It

was not only my one chance to fill in the blanks of my knowledge of the night at Cunningham's, but perhaps my one
chance to learn to talk to him at all. Yet I do not blame her for
protecting him.

The Polish clerk sniffled when he had finished reading the
charges, but the sniffle was more hay fever than compassion
since his face, when he turned to look at my father in a curious
gesture of clerkly interest, was blank as a ledger sheet.

There was a general pause in the courtroom as everyone,
pimps to bailiffs, seemed to avail themselves of the same
privilege of staring into a poor man's face. Only the moon
faced judge did not participate, first straightening the pale
lime shirt collar beneath his dark robes, and then gazing out
upon us, literally sighting the whole row of us. I felt the
judgement of his gaze against my face, and then the almond
eyes roamed on. Only when he reached my mother's face was
there a sense of compassion—a half-wink from one eye that
might have been an assurance or a nervous tic—as well as a
slight nod of approval at her stature of defiance. Or so it
seemed to me.

Our little civics lesson proceeded at a quick pace thereafter,
exactly as Maloney had sketched it, although with a surprise
or two.

First, the Assistant District Attorney, a high school classmate of my brother Pat, rose and asked permission to
approach the bench. Maloney gripped my father's arm,
squeezing with an I-told-you-so air of self-congratulation and
comradely largesse. As he squeezed my father's arm, he was
already moving up slightly on his toes in anticipation of the
next move.

"Counselor," the judge beckoned Maloney, and Maloney
stepped smartly from his tiptoes and up to the bench.

"Pshaw!" one of the pimps exclaimed, "Copping a plea!
These honkies got this sucker maneuvered. You be okay now,

Pops . . ." He saluted my father, who met this assurance with an embarrassed grin.

The Assistant DA, Maloney, and the judge whispered for a much longer time than it could conceivably have taken to agree on what they had already agreed on in his chambers. We all grew nervous and pensive; my father began to dance again, although this time it was surely pain from the time he had spent standing there. My mother was not watching any of this at all, since somewhere in the midst of the proceedings she had noticed a polyester-clad man with what was surely a reporter's notebook, and she concentrated now on scowling at him.

The huddle broke. I noticed as the judge began to speak that he had a single gold crown on a top front tooth. He spoke as though he had memorized his words, this time not looking at anyone in the courtroom, but gazing instead into the intermediate beyond.

"The People have moved that felony charges in this case be dropped, and counsel for the Defendant has indicated the defendant's willingness to enter a plea to lesser charges."

He pronounced the word, defendant, stressing the *ant*.

"Are these your wishes, Mr. Doyle?"

Since the judge was still addressing the beyond, my father did not at first know he was being spoken to.

"Mr. Doyle," the judge uttered the name with incredible gentleness, "are you feeling well, sir?"

"My back," my father said involuntarily, as if my mother had asked him the question in the kitchen.

"Well, please be seated, sir."

"That's right, Jim, this is your edifice," the pimp called out.

"And yours too, Mr. Bently-Jones," the judge parried with the pimp, "judging from the frequency of your visits here."

After the laughter of the bailiffs, other prisoners, and my brothers had settled, the judge repeated his original question.

"I guess so," my father replied, very weary now.

"You guess, Mr. Doyle?"

The whole room went tense. Maloney looked aghast.

"Yes," my father finally responded on cue.

"Well then, this court has entertained the motion of the People and hereby directs the Defendant to answer charges in Part B, Section V of the Traffic Court within twenty-four hours of this proceeding. Case dismissed."

There was a puzzled buzzing in our row and the whole room. Bently-Jones could not contain himself.

"Jesus, Pops, that mick lawyer of yours is something else! Copped a plea for running a red light, coming down from felony murder."

Bently-Jones laughed aloud, "Je-sus!"

The judge gavelled him, and—surprisingly—addressed my father.

"Mr. Doyle, may I be permitted a personal word?"

My father, dazed, granted the judge's request.

"Seek some counselling, sir," the judge said.

"I don't believe in *Sy-Ki-atrists*," my father said, pronouncing the word like he was beginning to recite the Greek alphabet.

"A clergyman then," the judge retorted, "A priest?"

"I'm not so sure that I believe in them either, your honor."

The judge nodded, and chewed his cheeks a moment. Then he bent slightly forward from the bench, intimating himself.

"Could you tell me how this happened, Mr. Doyle?" he asked.

My father said no, that he couldn't really tell.

If the judge was inquiring as to the particulars of my father's altercation with Black Peggy (as he surely was), then he is not alone in the ignorance which surrounds my father's crime. To this day no one except the principals themselves knows exactly what went on in the darkroom before my father marched Peggy out the door and down the block, a shotgun at her back.

A good deal is known of the events afterward, and as my

account suggests, of the events previous, but as for the lighting of the fuse itself, there is little known except what Deidre witnessed and participated in. It is as if their confrontation had come under the protection of a series of inviolable and enveloping tribal taboos, which among my people protect the interchanges between fathers and daughters (Peggy was partially that), and within bedrooms (even those abandoned and long given over to historical usage), and especially between man and woman (even aging Irish gentlemen and dark-eyed Black Irish childwomen).

This much is known: My father had recuperated for a full week after the events at Cunningham's, spending all his time in bed, with only brief excursions to the john and his darkroom. The second week he rose from his pallet and moved about the house and neighborhood, but he restricted his forays to the early morning when no Doyles were up, and spent the rest of the days and nights in the darkroom, even having his dinner brought up.

Peggy had come and gone as usual during this time, exchanging pleasantries with my father whenever she glimpsed him. Only my mother and The Prince had any long conversations with him. My mother's are, of course, protected; but The Prince has shared his own with all and sundry, although it sheds no light on what happened.

"He said he wanted to talk to me about the unions," Jimmy reported, "about the whole idea of trade-unionism and the nature of political thought. He said that: 'the nature of political thought.'"

"And?" I asked.

Jimmy screwed his face into an attempt to articulate a dim awareness. "I think he was really explaining to me what he thought was wrong with my arguing that we ought to blow him in as The Stranger."

"In so many words?"

"No, but he wanted to talk about how idealism and activism always clashed in the unions. I mean, I had started to tell him I was sorry about what happened, and he just winked and talked about idealism and activism. Idealism and activism, like that."

"You think he was saying you were wrong?" I asked.

Jimmy looked strangely at me. "No," he said, surprised, "I mean, it's pretty clear he was saying there are two ways to go about it, you know?"

I was not sure I did know. But something in Jimmy's report mingles with an odd feeling I have about my father's relationship to Peggy, and both lead me nearly to the point where I could believe my mother's somewhat paranoid theory that the whole shooting was something Peggy and my father had cooked up together in their talk in the darkroom.

"She's a scatterbrained thing with political thoughts, and the old coot likes her," my mother said. "I just bet they thought it would work."

"To do what?" I asked. "Bring out the rebels?"

"Maybe," she said, and she wouldn't say anymore. What Deidre heard that night was inconclusive on this point.

At any rate, one night during the second week, my father emerged from the darkroom and came down to the table where everyone was still lingering two hours after supper. He surprised the hell out of them, and he himself seemed surprised.

"Oh," he said, "I thought I heard Peg here."

"She's up in the john, you must have passed her on the way," Jim said.

"What is it?" my mother asked.

"Just something I wanted to show her," he said, turning to leave, "from the Irish documents." And he went back upstairs.

The Irish documents had arrived sometime in the second week and had been gathered up from the mail by my father before anyone knew they were there, or what exactly was in them. In fact, the only way the family knew at all before this night was that Deidre had noticed them stuffed away under a folded newspaper when she brought him supper one night.

"I only saw the Irish stamp on the envelope, and maybe a picture, although it could have been one of his . . . and some photocopy sheets with writing. He covered them up quickly when I asked."

"No wonder," my mother said. "The man has no privacy." She glared at Jimmy, who reported these events to me later.

"What did he say they were?" The Buddha asked.

"Irish Sweepstakes," Deidre answered, wrinkling her brow. "He was devilish about it. 'The biggest sweepstakes of them all!' he said."

Black Peggy, of course, did not come back down from the john that night until she came down under the escort of my father and my uncle's shotgun and Deidre shouting behind them. There had been some initial concern after my father went back upstairs, and Brendan and Deidre both had gone to stand at the bottom of the stairwell from time to time to see what they could hear, despite my mother's wishes.

All they heard was a mumble of talk, some early laughter from the both of them, occasional sounds of shuffling papers, and an interchange or two in only slightly raised voices. The conversations between Black Peggy and my father took over an hour. It was beginning to get dark outside but no one moved from the dinner table, neither to leave nor to dare a trip to the bathroom. My mother held them there.

Finally Deidre could stand it no longer and she went up.

"Mom grunted in disgust when I left the table," she told me, "But I had to go. I didn't want that child to hurt him."

She made this confession with a rueful laugh but no irony. I asked her to repeat what she had said.

"I didn't want her to hurt him," she repeated quietly, then cried. I felt awful about prying; I sometimes forgot that Deidre had her feelings. "Oh Edmund," she said, "sometimes you understand nothing, do you?"

I nodded. Sometimes I did not understand.

"She's really strong-willed," Deidre explained, "And Dad needs to be protected sometimes, if only from himself. All you men," she said, "all you damn Doyles . . . It's a holy war for you, but for us it's only life . . ."

She shook her head at me as if she despaired at my ever

understanding. She had made life sound like a wonderfully rich and complex thing, something I knew I could never understand as she did.

She had knocked at the darkroom door, she told me, and Peggy said to come in. They had heard her on the stairs and they were silent until she knocked. My father sat on the high stool with the gun across his lap, Peggy leaned idly against the wall opposite him.

"Stay where you are," my father ordered Deidre, "I don't want to hurt anybody."

"That's the normal function of a gun," Deidre said, and stepped between Peggy and the weapon.

My father did not move.

"Are you alright?" Deidre asked Peggy.

"Um . . ." Peggy said.

"I'll shield you to the door," Deidre said, "Stay behind me . . ." She edged toward the open door.

But Peggy did not move. Deidre reached the door alone and my father moved off the stool and between her and Peggy.

"Don't touch the gun," he said calmly, "I don't trust this thing . . ."

Even so Deidre reached toward Peggy.

"It's okay," Peggy said, slipping away.

"It most certainly is *not* okay!" Deidre shouted. "Just what do you expect to prove?"

I asked Deidre who she had addressed the question to, but she only shook her head. She did not know.

"Aw DeeDee . . ." my father crooned, "Don't you know there is nothing to prove? Don't you know that yet?"

"Don't you?" she taunted.

"I've got to clear our names," he said, "I've got to give us both a chance. Everything's gotten all out of whack and this little girl needs a chance . . ."

Deidre then challenged Peggy. "You think this is for you?" she asked, "You think you need a chance?"

162

Peggy looked away toward my father. He reached out and touched Deidre's still-outstretched hand. Then he moved behind Peggy. "There's a war on, DeeDee," he said, "There's always a war . . . We're just going for a walk, hon, that's all. We've got to show some people a thing or two."

He clicked something in the gun. Deidre moved away from the door. She told me she thought he had gone crazy.

"Mister Doyle knows what he's doing," Peggy said, "I'm really not afraid as long as nobody messes him up . . ."

Deidre nodded. They went past her and down the hall.

"He was close enough for me to touch," she told me, "I could have grabbed the gun . . . But it was my father, Edmund, my father. I couldn't touch him . . . Besides I believed when Peggy said he knew what he was doing."

Still she had shouted after them.

"And what are you going to show them?"

"Something more than a hole in the ground," my father shouted back. "All we Irish ever wanted was a fair fight and a good name!"

"And what will that gain you?" Deidre cried out again. But her courage gave out then and she cried.

Peggy moaned in distress, hearing Deidre cry. My father shouted, "I told you!" and they went down the stairs.

Downstairs everyone heard the footsteps and the shouts, the distress cry from Peggy, my father's "I told you!" There was a mass exit toward the front hall landing. The desperado and his hostage were coming down the first flight of stairs.

"He's got Uncle Pat's gun!" Jimmy cried.

"But he doesn't know how to use it, I'll grab him!" Brendan shouted, and made for the stairs.

"Don't be an ass!" my mother slapped Brendan. "You'll hurt him again, and he's just recovering from your brother's trick."

Brendan was largely correct about my Uncle Pat's gun, although the picture window to the rear of our neighborhood Marine Trust branch can attest to the fact that my father was finally able to successfully discharge the weapon. Previous to that, however, the shotgun had only been discharged twice since it had come to our house after Pat's death. The first time, in a target shooting episode on my mother's sister's farm, had resulted in absolutely no damage to a cardboard carton. Brendan and my father had set the carton well beyond the range of the spray of birdshot, which dispersed itself harmlessly and noisily in the back yard. The second time had been less planned, and the birdshot did a fair job of blowing three feet of plaster from the lathe in the darkroom. After that accidental toppling of the weapon, my mother insisted that it remain unloaded, despite my father's protestations that Uncle Pat had a point about the need to defend the household.

After my mother had thwarted Brendan's charge, the rest of the family held back. The only one to speak was my mother.

"Matt, what's going on?" she asked.

"I'm sorry," he said, then shook his head as if he was unable to explain more.

"We'll be alright," Peggy said quietly. "Don't anyone be stupid. We'll be alright."

And on that note they marched through the front hallway and out into the night, Black Peggy, the hostage priestess, and Matt Doyle, the Connaught chieftain, linked by an unreliable shotgun and a common understanding of the task before them.

There are zones of acceptable madness within our neighborhood. Like conic sections each roughly encompassing a block of houses, they offer general sanctuary for mad acts within them, submitting the perpetrators to no jurisdiction other than that of gossip and an occasional visit from either the Irish firemen or a bored squad car. Thus, when we were younger and the Kollik's, the crazy Ukranian couple across the street, used to come home drunk and fight, with Mrs. K. throwing burning garbage sacks out on the lawn, as she screamed threats to each of us neighbors by name; there was no reckoning other than talk and the daylight glances from neighbors who knew that this dumpy woman with her string-sack of groceries became a witch by midnight.

My father marched Peggy through zone after zone of such sanctuary on his way to the bank branch. If anywhere along that march he had paused and reconsidered, even discharged the gun at anything other than Peggy or another human, he would never have gone to court.

I can't believe he didn't know this; and thus can't believe he didn't intend to go the full distance with this impossible and ironic act. Even had he entered the parking lot behind the bank directly from Indian Church, foregoing the march through the lights of Seneca Street, past the front of the bank, Kimaid and Mattar's clothing store, and Sattler Drugs, and into the notice of whatever passing motorist it was who alerted the police; most likely he would have escaped un-apprehended. For vandalism of any public kind, but especial-ly vandalism against a bank, is not something the inhabitants of our village are liable to go out of their way to see prose-cuted.

But my father took the public route, attracting not only the attention of the public-spirited motorist but also a parade of onlookers and witnesses—including a court kid or too—be-fore he stopped at the rear of the bank, bade Peggy move up toward the window, and pumped the gun.

Then, according to eye-witnesses, who by this time included my brothers, my father sighted along the barrel to where Peggy stood, lowered the weapon for a moment again as he mopped sweat from his brow, then shouted.

"I told you, didn't I?" he intoned in his wonderful deep voice.

Peggy nodded.

He lifted the barrel and sighted again.

"Get the hell out of the way," he said. Whether this was to the onlookers or Peggy is a matter of dispute, but Peggy availed herself of the, at least implied, invitation.

Then, just as the scream of the squad cars was heard, and

the first of their lights began to swirl against the house fronts on Buffum and in the far end of the plaza, he shouted, "Goddamn the banks!" and fired the gun, the picture window exploding in a neat thump and a tinkle of glass shards, all of the glass blown inward.

The onlookers waited a moment to see if he would charge into the gaping hole in the bank, then obeyed the instructions of the policemen in the late arriving cars, who told them to move on. Meanwhile the first of the policemen arrested him, while another picked up the gun from where he had tossed it aside (surely in terror of their enthusiasm), and a third crawled into the bank looking for some way to turn off the jangling alarm bell.

The charged him with attempted murder and bank theft.

The judge asked a final, quiet question.

"Am I to understand that you owe no money to that bank, Mr. Doyle? No mortgages, loans, anything?"

My father nodded silently.

The judge grinned.

"A gesture, was it? Goddamn . . ." He had failed to muffle the last imprecation, and he looked chagrined. "You have a fine family, Mr. Doyle," he said, gesturing to the row of us. "Go home to them when this is over, okay?"

"I don't drink," my father said, answering an unasked question.

The judge grinned again, and gestured to the Polish clerk, who ushered Maloney and my father out and began to call the next case.

We all filed out of our row behind them, wardkeeper attorney and old Fenian, ready for the next journey to the Traffic Court, and my father's final judgement, at least in the official realms of this world. As soon as she reached the aisle, my mother buttonholed Maloney and pointed to the reporter. Maloney nodded and went to talk to the polyester man. My mother took my father's hand. In Traffic Court, my father pleaded guilty to violating two ordinances: public mischief and discharging a firearm. He was fined and put on probation as I've already noted.

As in the way with most rebellions in minor provinces, there was nothing about these violations or his trial in the newspapers. Maloney, my mother, and the public good had struck a bargain with the press.

Epilogue

I left at night, a few days after the trial, taking a taxi to the airport for the night flight. I was looking forward to the calm of the flight: few passengers, the most of them either off-duty airline crews, or economical types, or people with somewhere to go in the late night when we would land. The anonymity of this group of strangers seemed a welcome alternative to the blurring interconnections and complexities of the Doyles.

Even so, I was struck by a feeling of betrayal, of disloyalty, in my wanting to go. To act as if I were free of them.

My father saw me off, waiting on the porch with me until the taxi rounded the corner and began to scan the house numbers with his light. It was obviously an unusual thing for us, to be seen off by only one person, and without the crowd of farewells. We were both aware of how odd it was, as if the others had burdened this time of ours with their unusual absence. We did not know how to act, or what we were expected to say. We stood there on the porch, my bag between us, both smoking cigarettes, neither thinking to sit.

"What will you do next?" he asked.

He was only trying to make talk, but the question took on a laden quality, a sense of closure.

"Home," I said.

"You mean Japan?" he asked, as if prompting me.

I sensed sadness in his voice, and I knew that I had let him down by not going through with the usual delusional script.

But I, too, was sad. That he continued to allow, even encourage, this joke—this delusion—of mine, calling Michigan, Japan, denying and inventing at the same time, saddened me. There was something weary and sad about each usage of ours which he assumed, whether using the word, "bummer," in the delicate adjectival way he did, or arguing with Brendan about baseball, or calling Jimmy "The Prince" along with us. He gave up more than he gave us with each of these instances, and I did not want him to give up any more.

His eyes used to smile and mock me whenever he humored my insistence by using the joke name in the past. But that night he said it blankly, forlorn, as if he wished it were truly so foreign, so filled with alien hope.

I considered saying, "No, just home. It's not Japan anymore for me," but the taxi came around the corner and, as I reached for the bag between us, the driver's light flashed full upon my father's face. In the light it was dreamy, and old, his eyes were misted. It had been a tough spring.

"Yes, to Japan," I said.

His hand had beaten mine to the bag and he insisted on carrying it down to the cab. We embraced formally in the street. He gripped my hand, unwilling to let me go.

"We had a bachelor uncle in Ireland," he said, "You and I. He was a Cuddy not a Doyle. They called him Paddy Stink. He drove his cart into Dublin one morning, full of stinking fat silvery fish. A whole day's catch. He drove his cart right up Parkgate Street into Phoenix Park and up to the Vice-Regent's lawn where he shovelled them off, the whole cart load, before the soldier's clubbed him off.

"The British, you see, had taken his livelihood from him, and he wanted them to see what he had lost . . ."

170

He smiled sheepishly in the streetlight. The cabbie gunned his engine impatiently.

"It was no Boston Tea Party," my father said, releasing my hand. "But I imagine those fish shone some on that green lawn, don't you see?"

I nodded. He patted my shoulder.

"Go on now," he said, "It was only something I wanted you to know, and I just found it out myself. I'm just passing it on for Paddy Stink. You see, he had no sons . . ."

He was waving in the street as the cab pulled away, silver in his eyes.

We had all lost something, the promise of our new world in those months. Our America is a sodden land now, a lapsing kingdom, being pulled down by its overseers—the protty aristocracy and their oil baron henchmen. It is like a travelling puppet show which has ended its run, worn both its backdrops and marionettes to fraying. And there is no other land for us to move to now, the last of the tribes of Israel, Connaught, and the Iroquois Confederacy. Not even my own adopted and imagined land will do, this buddhist science fiction Japan of the post-industrial age, where *sunyata* and yawning chaos are seen as one thing in the faces of the silent commuters on the jammed silver trains speeding at hundreds of miles per hour past rural gardens and ancestor altars and the thin, dark trees with Shinto paper prayers tied to their limbs like dry, white leaves.

Goodbye, Dad, I thought.

But there was no goodbye, of course. He called within hours of when I arrived home. I had let myself in at dawn and walked down the hall to see Thomas. To sit in his room watching him sleep, stir, and then finally awaken, wide-eyed and a little scared to see me staring there. We went in to see Mary. She asked about my father.

"He asked me, while we were waiting on the porch for the cab, why you hadn't come," I said, then corrected myself when I saw the alarm in her eyes. She had wanted to come.

"No," I said, "His exact words were, 'Too bad Mary and Thomas couldn't come to see us.' "

"We can," she said, "Soon."

"I told him it wasn't exactly a vacation."

My father called after we had eaten breakfast, just as I was about to take a nap. He wanted to make sure I got back alright; he realized that he had forgotten to tell me that he was glad I had been there; he wanted me to tell Mary and Thomas hello for him.

"You want to talk to them?" I asked.

"Not just now, Edmund," he said, in the soft and penitant voice he had lately assumed.

I realized that I had been reading the paper before me as we talked. I felt like a proper traitor. I hadn't even been able to watch with him.

But it is not that call I remember. Or rather say, will remember; for he is most certainly not dead, and the house continues to churn its complex dramas. The Prince and Black Peggy are no closer or farther apart than ever, Moira's children fail and get well in cycles, and so on and on. There is no end to it all.

The call I will remember came months after, in late November, the day in fact of the first snow of that season. It was one of my father's "wondering how you all are, haven't heard from you lately" calls. No more significant than any number of other calls, except perhaps that it came in mid-afternoon, not his usual calling time. I had conducted my part of the conversation somewhat better than I usually do. Recalling enough of the little household and child events to interest him, responding to his conversational cues, asking about his health, bidding him to give my love to everyone there, forgetting only to ask him about the genealogy and his progress.

When we finished, however, I realized how stupid and slow and satisfying my realizations ultimately are. After the call I understood suddenly (stopped still, standing by the table in a daze) that his call were genuine attempts to be known for and as himself. No more or less.

They were a series of greetings, a late reckoning from him to match his constant, early farewells.

There was a certain amount of peace in the knowledge that real intimacy, any catching up, was impossible for us. At least, I thought, I realized that before it was too late. Maybe I too could hone my attention to him.

Thinking back through the call, I recalled how we each had paused from time to time, silent, as if about to tell the truth about everything. Each time we resumed the empty catalogue of telephones: no news, no news, no news. I had watched the white field behind our house in the pauses, snow over timothy grass and burdock.

Sometime in those days—it may have even been that same day—I took Thomas for a walk in the powdery snow, past the horses, and up along the path to the neighbor's pond, his mitten held in my bare, freezing hand.

We came upon a string of wild grapes in the aspens near the pond—the bareness of the trees only then disclosing them, strung from tree to tree like garlands. They were incredibly sweet, dark small things, no more really than skin, stones, and a thick sugar juice. Thomas and I were stained with them, his mouth and hands black-purple, his hands frozen from discarding the mittens.

The winter comes in with sweetness, I thought. All turned to sugar. The last apples from our tree were also unbearably sweet when we were able to find one unmarred and uninfested.

Near the pond we found a sole dandelion, close to the earth, hardly a stem. It seemed a brave survival, this persistence in the face of winter. Thomas asked excitedly if he could pick the flower, and when I did not answer, he did, crushing it gold in his palm, dancing along at my side.

About the Author

Michael Joyce lives and works in Michigan, with his wife Martha and his son Eamon.

Design by Brenn Lea Pearson.
Typeset in Baskerville by
Kachina Typesetting, Inc., Tempe, Arizona,
printed at Thomson-Shore, Inc.,
Dexter, Michigan.

John Enright made this book.

The support of many
made it possible.